3

412. 609 LILI BAT

The Prince of Wales in Garter robes, 1799. The Prince Regent not only was the greatest of the royal patrons of the arts but was himself a discerning participant. 'He adorned all the subjects he touched', in the words of the sophisticated Princess Lieven.

Introduction

George IV was Regent only from 1811 until 1820, but the term 'Regency', to which his title was given, is usually taken to cover the period from 1794, when the ideas which gave rise to the style began to ferment, until the accession of Queen Victoria in 1837. The fashionable, pleasure-loving Prince took great interest in all the arts and was a prodigious and discerning collector of pictures, furniture, porcelain and statuary. He was a compulsive builder and an enthusiastic promoter of new ideas in architecture, town planning and technology and it was only to be expected that he would hold strong views on the changing ideas in landscape gardening which preoccupied people at the turn of the century.

Eighteenth-century taste was aristocratic, sanctioned by such arbiters as Lord Burlington, within a strong philosophical framework provided by Shaftesbury, Addison, Pope, Hogarth and Burke. Regency taste was more flexible and intuitive and embraced a much wider and more democratic society. In place of pediments, porticoes and Palladian stairways, Regency houses had striped canopies, verandahs, balconies and ornamental ironwork and, as an accompaniment to the light playfulness of the architecture, more 'dressed' grounds near the house, with sinuous shrubberies, flowerbeds, trellis and ornate garden seats. Garden design no longer depended on extent of property for effect, as in the days of 'Capability' Brown, and estate priorities had to be reassessed to meet the cost of living in the Napoleonic Wars and increased taxation.

Landscaping and gardening were increasingly seen as separate concepts and, even though Humphry Repton was still working on such large-scale landscape improvements as Woburn and Stoneleigh, he came to see the garden as a frame for the landscape, which should be separated from the park by a fence or a parapet. The new 'upstart wealth', as Repton called profits from war contracts and fund-holding, usually wanted instant results rather than waiting for a landscape to mature, as the old landed interest had been prepared to do.

There was a new connection between house and garden through conservatories and flower corridors; interior decoration and trellised verandahs complemented each other, fluted curtains, flowerstands and flouncing shrubberies matching the elegance of Regency costume. Jane Austen, who perfectly captures the more relaxed style of Regency living, has only to place a heroine, reading romantic poetry or playing a seductive harp, by a French window opening on to a flowery shrubbery, for her to catch any man's heart.

The chief exponents of the new Regency gardening style were Humphry Repton, Henry Phillips, J. B. Papworth, John Nash, who extended it to town planning, W. T. Aiton, J. C. Loudon in his early days and William Sawrey Gilpin, who made a brave attempt at reviving landscape gardening, notably at Scotney Castle, as late as 1840, when Victorian ideas of horticulture had taken over. Regency ideas were taken to Europe through Repton's books and by Prince Pückler-Muskau, who was a most informative Regency traveller and, having met Nash in England, carried out his ideas on landscape planning on his own estate and wrote a book on the subject. Regency gardening, adapted by the American landscape architect A. J. Downing, took root across the Atlantic.

Although Regency gardening was a distinctive style and widely used, few examples of it can be identified today. A country house album will usually contain an eighteenth-century engraving showing the mansion on an extensive lawn bounded by a ha-ha and grazing herds and a landscaped lake beyond. Next in sequence may well be a photograph of the Victorian family taking tea on a terrace in the midst of fountains and highly decorative bedding-out schemes. Unless the intervening period had caught the eye of an early nineteenth-century illustrator, such as Ackermann, there will be no record of what the Regency garden looked like before it was refashioned in the Victorian period. Some restorations of Regency-style gardens are now being undertaken and it is most fortunate that the major one should be at the Royal Pavilion, Brighton, which is most intimately associated with the Prince Regent.

Regency architecture

The inspiration of the Picturesque

Palladian houses, in the eighteenth century, had stood foursquare in the landscape, rising up out of extensive lawns, but, following the theory of the Picturesque, promulgated by Richard Payne Knight and Uvedale Price in 1794, there was a new desire to make buildings compose in the scenery as they did in landscape paintings. In his extended *Essay on the Picturesque* in 1798, Uvedale Price called for a new breed of 'painter-architect', who would 'accommodate his building to the scenery, not make that give way to the building'. Payne Knight had already demonstrated how this could be achieved when he planned his asymmetrical house at Downton in 1774 to compose with its rugged Herefordshire landscape (see pages 2-3).

An avid art-collector, Knight owned no fewer than 273 drawings by Claude, which he studied intently, and encouraged other landowners intent on building to study Claude and Poussin, in whose pictures classical and Gothic buildings were 'naturalised' in the landscape. John Nash, who had become acquainted with Price and Knight early in his career, was soon to become the acknowledged master of picturesque architecture, particularly when Humphry Repton, the landscape gardener, became his partner from 1795 to

Luscombe Castle, Devon (1799): a picturesque composition by Nash and Repton.

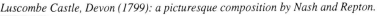

1800, and together they produced such delightfully picturesque compositions as Luscombe in Devon.

At the same time as promoting picturesque architecture Knight had poured scorn on eighteenth-century landscaping in the Brownian style in his poem 'The Landscape', published in 1794, the same year as Price's *Essay on the Picturesque*. For 'The Landscape' Thomas Hearne, who had already painted twelve watercolours of Downton, made two illustrations to make a comparison between a Palladian house in an improved smooth Brownian-type landscape and the natural picturesque alternative, which had unmistakable echoes of Knight's Claude drawings and his own irregular Downton Castle.

From castle to cottage

Medieval and Tudor buildings with their intricate skylines were consciously imitated; only such irregular shapes could be related to scenery and compose into picturesque masses, giving contrast and light and shade effects. In 1798 James Malton, who was much influenced by Price's *Essay*, went beyond manorial buildings and

Woodbine Cottage near Torquay: a bathing cottage and machine for Miss Johnes of Croft Castle.

Houghton Lodge: a fishing retreat by the river Test, an early cottage orné. A far cry from a genuine cottage with 'calm desires that need but little room'.

made a study of the humbler *British Cottage Architecture*, as 'an attempt to perpetuate on Principle, that peculiar mode of Building, which was originally the effect of Chance'. Overhanging eaves, lean-tos, weatherboarding, tall chimneys and rustic porches on cottages were seen to be every bit as irregular and picturesque as castle architecture. Malton pointed out that cottages, as well as castles, were also featured in landscape paintings, particularly in scenes by Dutch painters.

These picturesque vernacular cottages could be built, not only for peasants and farmers, but as 'retreats for gentlemen'. In 1802 in *Designs for Villas* James Malton suggested that a gentleman should have several such villas in 'several distinct neighbourhoods – a hunting box at one place, a shoot-box at another: with a cottage for the amusement of angling: as also dwellings on the sea shore for marine advantages'. Such cottage retreats usually had, like Houghton beside the river Test in Hampshire, stables and other outbuildings. Robert Lugar in his *Architectural Sketches for Cottages, Rural Dwellings and Villas*, published in 1805, seems to have been the first architect to use the expression 'cottage orné' for such a cottage-style affluent dwelling.

Nuneham Courtenay: the village removed to its present site in 1761 in the making of Lord Harcourt's landscaped garden.

The cult of the cottage

Jane Austen, writing in the new century, showed that cottages, defined in Dr Johnson's *Dictionary* as 'mean habitations', were by then, in the relaxed Regency mode of living, permissible as main residences. Robert Ferrars in *Sense and Sensibility* was 'excessively fond of a cottage; there is always so much comfort, so much elegance about them... I advise everybody who is going to build, to build a cottage. My friend Lord Courtland came to me the other day on purpose to ask my advice, and laid before me three different plans of Bonomi's. I was to decide on the best of them. "My dear Courtland", said I, immediately throwing them all in the fire, "do not adopt either of them, but by all means build a cottage." And that, I fancy, will be the end of it.'

Robert Ferrars's ideas about rearranging the cottage rooms for genteel supper parties and card tables as required were a far cry from the genuine cottage life style with Oliver Goldsmith's 'calm desires that need but little room'. The ornamental garden for the new Regency cottage was also remote from the genuine cottage garden, which was a functional space for barrels, ladders, hurdles and produce which was part of the economy of the cottage. Covering the house with creepers, however, was copied from a genuine 'effect of chance' in cottage architecture and many pattern books for cottages ornés showed walls 'adapted to receive trained foliage'.

The removal of peasant cottages from the landlord's park had often been the first stage in eighteenth-century landscape improvements, which Oliver Goldsmith had condemned in his poem 'The Deserted Village' in 1770, having seen one such village, Nuneham Courtenay, near Oxford, being demolished in 1761 in the making of Lord Harcourt's landscaped garden. More benevolent ideas, after the French Revolution, condemned Lord Harcourt's high-handed action. Uvedale Price pointed out that improved picturesque cottages could benefit the rural poor and at the same time embellish the park scenery. 'It is possible', he continued, 'that those whom all the affecting images and pathetic touches of Goldsmith would not have restrained from destroying a village, may even be induced to build one to show their taste.'

Price had been led to believe by Goldsmith's poem that the inhabitants of 'sweet Auburn' had been sent into beggary, prostitution or emigration, whereas they had been rehoused in what the Poet Laureate, William Whitehead, called 'happier mansions, warm and dry', outside the landscaped park. Admittedly the new Nuneham Courtenay was not the picturesque hamlet that Price envisaged,

The ornamental dairy at Blaise Castle, 1803.

Blaise Hamlet, by Francis Danby: a landlord's picturesque hamlet, soon after it was built, in sharp contrast to Nuneham Courtenay, strung out along the turnpike. (Courtesy of City of Bristol Museums and Art Gallery.)

Wreaths of smoke from the village. Repton's Red Book for Stoneleigh Abbey, 1809.

Adlestrop, Gloucestershire: bath-house for a member of Jane Austen's family.

Endsleigh, Devon: children's cottage and garden, 1814.

clustering round a village green, but was strung out, like a London street, along the turnpike, its inn bearing the arms of the noble benefactor.

Blaise Hamlet

A truly picturesque hamlet of nine cottages for family retainers, built to a high standard around a green, was created in 1810 at Blaise Hamlet near Bristol, where the landlord, John Scandrett Harford, lived up to Price's aspirations of an owner showing both benevolence and taste on his estate. John Nash and Repton's sons, George Stanley and John Adey, had already demonstrated that picturesque estate architecture could provide just as much interest in the landscape as ruins and follies when they built a delightful thatched ornamental dairy for Harford at Blaise Castle in 1803.

The thatched stone cottages at Blaise Hamlet, also built by Nash and Repton's sons, were situated in a woodland setting on a green with a pump and sundial. A sloping roof covered the privy, providing both convenience and picturesque shading, and a variety of different chimneys gave additional picturesque effect. Neat hedges and garlands of clematis, roses and honeysuckles hung over the cottages named Vine, Sweet Briar, Oak, Circular, Dial, Jessamine, Rose, Diamond and Double. Every consideration was given to the comfort and privacy of the occupants, each porch being arranged so that no door could be seen from any other. Privacy was short-lived, however, as the hamlet appeared in every guide book and even Prince Pückler-Muskau visited on his Regency tour of England and commented approvingly.

Repton and the rustic style

Repton, who disapproved of artificial ruins, commended rustic buildings, for a variety of uses, in his landscape improvements: thatched ornamental dairies, gamekeepers' or woodmen's cottages, often with a useful garden seat in the wall for walkers in the park, or lodges with tree trunk columns at the entrance to the drive. Even without a visual architectural presence, the curling smoke, marking the preparation of the peasant's evening meal, would add a note of cheerfulness to the park scene. After Wordsworth's 'Lines written a few miles above Tintern Abbey' in 1798, 'wreaths of smoke sent up, in silence, from among the trees' were romantic as well as picturesque.

The Reptons also designed picnic cottages, such as the Thornery at Woburn Abbey, or a delightful little ladies' bath-house by the stream at Adlestrop for the family. Repton would not have agreed with Robert Ferrars in *Sense and Sensibility*, however, that a person of rank, such as Lord Courtland, should build his residence in the cottage style. Repton's professional livelihood depended on a healthy conservatism and respect for the nobility, who should reside preferably in the seats of their ancestors or appropriately dignified modern mansions with a large acreage to be landscaped. Repton's own cottage at Hare Street in Essex had Regency trellis features but was not in cottage vernacular.

Endsleigh, Devon
Repton's ingenious solution for the sixth Duke of Bedford, who asked him, in 1809, to provide him with a picturesque lodge for pheasant shooting and salmon fishing on the Tamar, was to design, with his sons, a ducal Blaise Hamlet. Endsleigh, near Tavistock, was to consist of a series of detached picturesque buildings for the Duke and Duchess, the children and the servants linked by verandahs and arcades. Repton's ideas for accommodating a 'noble proprietor' on holiday were not adopted but the large lodge, later built by Wyatville, with irregular elevations achieved the same picturesque effect.

Repton's proposals in his Red Book of 1814 for the landscaping of Endsleigh were, however, mainly carried out; these included extensive plantations and walks, a weir on the Tamar, a flower-festooned verandah, a pool in Dairy Dell and a long terrace walk with a conservatory banked with flowers on a pebbled retaining wall. From an alcove the parents could watch their children sailing their boats on a pond in a flower garden with a fountain in the middle. A fire was lit in the woodman's cottage, even in his absence, so that, as recommended, the curling smoke would enliven the park scenery.

Rural architecture and the ferme ornée
John Plaw, who is best-known for the circular house on Belle Isle, Lake Windermere, was one of the first to publish pattern books for ornamental cottages and rural dwellings, which became so popular in the early nineteenth century. He was much influenced by Repton's books, from which he frequently quoted, and maintained that he designed his houses to harmonise with the scenery.

He seems to have caught the moment when one landlord was so enthused by a scenically picturesque estate cottage being built for a worker that he wanted to live in it himself. Writing in 1800, Plaw reported that 'the building was originally begun for a cottager or a hind and to be visited occasionally, but by degrees grew into favour and was finished in this manner and is now the residence of the family'.

Leigh Park: Regency farmhouse, now a tea room in the Staunton Country Park, Havant. (Watercolour by J. F. Gilbert.)

Stoke Farm, Buckinghamshire: a ferme ornée with a colonnade of unbarked stems. (Ackermann's 'Views of Country Seats', 1830. By courtesy of the Bodleian Library, Oxford.)

West Cottage: a Sussex seaside farmhouse 'elevated into a cottage'.

John Plaw, who had a practice in the Southampton area, seems to have invented the architectural concept of the ferme ornée. Southcote and Shenstone, who had two of the earliest eighteenth-century fermes ornées, saw them as Arcadian landscapes, where the farm could be seen as an idealised picture from a perimeter walk. John Plaw in his *Ferme Ornée or Rural Improvements*, in 1795, illustrated how a whole farm complex could be 'calculated for landscape and picturesque effects' with a Gothic farmhouse, dog kennels, paddock sheds, shepherds' huts, etc. One such picturesque edifice, Plaw suggested, might be built on wheels and moved at pleasure.

An interesting example of a Regency ferme ornée was built at Leigh Park, near Havant, where the farmhouse and its oval garden and some of the Gothic pig styes, etc, are being restored. The owner himself did not live there, however, but saw it as part of his rural amusements. Appropriately, now that it is open to the public it has become a farm trail. More often, as at Stoke Farm in Buckinghamshire, which Ackermann thought 'may be termed a ferme ornée', the farmhouse was embellished by 'a rustic colonnade with unbarked stems of trees around which grow roses and jessamine' and continued to operate as a farm.

In a reverse process an old farmhouse might be converted into a

Strawberry Hill, Twickenham. Strawberry Hill was very influential on Regency Gothic, particularly on cottages ornés.

Fonthill by James Wyatt. (From J. Rutter, 'Delineations of Fonthill and Its Abbey', 1823.)

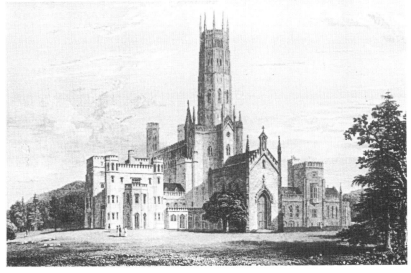

View from the prospect cottage at Matlock, built for Admiral Collingwood, second in command at Trafalgar.

cottage orné with Regency additions and cast off any pretensions to agriculture. The literal change from farmhouse to cottage can often be traced in deeds. One working Sussex farmhouse by the sea, which was called West House in 1760, was bought by a sailor with his prize money after the end of the Napoleonic Wars and converted into a picturesque seaside cottage orné with Strawberry Hill windows and fashionable Roman cement to cover the brick and flint; it was then renamed West Cottage. The ever observant Jane Austen, who had an eye for such fashionable foibles, comments in *Persuasion* that a farmhouse in Uppercross had recently been 'elevated' into a cottage with a verandah and pretty windows.

Strawberry Hill influence

Horace Walpole was the first person to live in a would-be Gothic house, when he started to build his famous Strawberry Hill at Twickenham in 1747. The 'Abbot of Strawberry' had a lifelong love-affair with Gothic and all it stood for in his imagination. Strawberry Hill was composed as a picture in the Thames landscape long before Picturesque theory had been formulated and twenty years before Payne Knight had thought of his castellated Downton. It remains as a lasting memorial to rococo Gothic, which would

Woolbrook Cottage, now the Royal Glen Hotel, Sidmouth, Devon.

give rise, fifty years later, to the full-blooded monastic Gothic of Fonthill for the arch-romantic William Beckford, the author of *Vathek*. James Wyatt's fantastic Fonthill collapsed in 1825 but his abbey-style Ashridge, with its huge staircase tower, begun in 1808, has lived on to become a Gothic management college.

For more modest houses, particularly for cottages ornés, it was Walpole's windows that became the most fashionable feature of the widespread Strawberry Hill cult. Prospect cottages in the Lakes or Peaks seemed to lend themselves to Strawberry Hill, rather than vernacular cottage architecture, and picturesque scenery looked well through Strawberry Hill windows, often with small coloured panes, as Admiral Collingwood, second in command at Trafalgar, found in retirement at Matlock.

Sidmouth still has numbers of delightful Regency cottages ornés. Woolbrook Cottage, superbly 'elevated' from a farmhouse, now the Royal Glen Hotel, is an excellent example of the influence of Strawberry Hill. It was converted for the Prince Regent's brother, the Duke of Kent, in 1819, and here he brought the infant Victoria

Opposite: 'Fragments on the Theory and Practice of Landscape Gardening', 1816, showing the ancient cedar parlour contrasted with the modern living room.

to stay. Apart from the salubrity of the sea breezes, Devon enabled him to escape his creditors. One of its most interesting features is the verandah leading from the upstairs drawing room on to a raised grass terrace, linking the interior of the house to the garden in the new way that the Regency life style favoured. Francis Goodwin, giving a plan for a verandah in his *Rural Architecture*, felt that it 'may be said to take the room itself abroad, for when rendered so attractive as it may be here, it would frequently seduce the work-table or the reading-table into its own neutral ground, between the house and the open air'.

Regency informality

The house and the garden became increasingly united in the Regency period, beginning with what Repton called 'the modern improvement, borrowed from the French, of folding glass doors opening into a garden, by which the effect in a room is like that of a tent or marquee, and in summer delightful'. Repton was anxious to adapt the interior of the house to this more informal kind of living. In *Fragments*, published in 1814, he illustrated his ideas of relaxed domesticity.

No More the Cedar Parlour's formal gloom
With dullness chills, 'tis now the Living Room
Where guests, to whim or taste or fancy true,
Scattered in groups their different plans pursue.

Repton had already expressed these ideas in the Red Book for Stoneleigh in 1809 when he condemned 'cedar parlours mentioned in the works of Richardson where society existed without the Music, the Pamphlet or the newspapers of the present day' and he rejoiced in 'the litter and confusion of chairs, tables, books and instruments in a modern library and living room'. Stoneleigh was Jane Austen's mother's ancestral home and she must have known the Red Book presented to her cousin by Repton, whose fees she revealed were 5 guineas a day. In *Persuasion* she writes of one household's efforts to provide itself with 'the proper air of confusion' that Repton's Regency living demanded. 'Younger generations of Musgraves were gradually persuading their parents to give their old-fashioned square parlour the proper air of confusion by a grand pianoforte, a harp, flowerstands and little tables placed in every direction. The portraits stared down in astonishment.'

There was no limit to the garden features that could be brought into the cottage orné by romantics in a scenic situation. J. B. Papworth describes the embellishments in the home of two ladies 'in the neighbourhood of the Lakes':

'The little hall and staircase are decorated with trellising, composed of light lath and wicker basket-work, very neatly executed and painted a dark green, flower-stands and brackets are attached at various parts, from bottom to the top of the staircase...the walls are everywhere adorned with them, and some are trained over the trellis of the ceilings, whence they hang in festoons and unite their branches.'

The interiors of Regency town houses

The extension of a garden room opening out from the house gave a new dimension to fashionable entertainment and a new type of entrepreneur set up to exploit the opportunities. Interior decorators and florist contractors set up to provide scented floral displays and potted plants for gala nights in marquees leading from the house to the illuminated garden. Maria Edgeworth in *The Absentee*, published in 1812, describes a supper room with trellised paper, in Grosvenor Square, 'with scenery to imitate Vauxhall opening on to a greenhouse lighted with coloured lamps in which a band played'. Attending a ball in a London house in 1827, Prince Pückler-Muskau commented that 'the whole garden was covered over and divided into large rooms which were hung with draperies of rose-coloured muslin, enormous ornamental mirrors and numerous chandeliers and perfumed with every kind of flower'.

Pitshanger Manor, Ealing

Sir John Soane, who in 1794 built his own house in Lincoln's Inn Fields, now the Sir John Soane Museum, excelled in designing ceilings which gave the effect of fluted tents suspended above the walls. He felt the breakfast parlour with its domed starfish ceiling, inset mirrors and indirect lighting presented 'a series of those fanciful effects which constitute the poetry of architecture'. In 1800 he built himself a country villa, Pitshanger Manor, with many of the same effects he had used at Lincoln's Inn Fields.

Pitshanger Manor, which is now part of Ealing and functions as a museum, has been restored, with its starfish ceiling patterned with trellis work and flower sprays, inspired by the one in the London house. Soane thought that enfilade mirrors gave 'magical effects' but a visitor to Pitshanger Manor mistook them for a corridor and injured himself so severely that some of them were removed. The breakfast room opened on to a conservatory, which ran the length of the building, with sash windows to the floor, partly of coloured glass. Soane described it as 'enriched with antique cinerary urns, sepulchral vases, statues...vines and odiferous plants; the whole

Pitshanger Manor, Ealing: Soane's breakfast room opening on to the conservatory. (J. M. Gandy, 1802.)

Keats House, Hampstead: a Regency maisonette.

producing a succession of beautiful effects, particularly when seen by moonlight, or when illuminated, and the lawn enriched with company enjoying the delights of cheerful society'.

Keats House, Hampstead

John Keats went to live at Wentworth Place in 1818 after his consumptive brother, whom he had nursed throughout his illness, died. The house, which belonged to his friend Charles Brown, was a Regency maisonette with a shared front door and garden. Keats had a special love for the garden adjoining Hampstead Heath, in which he wrote his 'Ode to a Nightingale'. The mingling of cottage gardens and heathland inspired much of Keats's poetry – sweet peas peeping over walls, laburnums and lilacs, trellised roses and mossy-trunked fruit trees with the heath and its gorse and pines and wild flowers in the background. Even on Mount Latmos Endymion is surrounded by Hampstead harebells, violets, daisies and scented limes. Nature spilled over into Hampstead gardens and the nightingale that nested at Wentworth Place apparently made no distinction.

Keats's feelings for the garden were heightened by the arrival of Fanny Brawne, to whom he became secretly engaged, in the nextdoor unit. In the 'Ode to Psyche' his love for Fanny and their delight in the shared garden are immortalised.

A rosy sanctuary will I dress
With the wreath'd trellis of a working brain
With buds, and bells, and stars without a name,
With all the gardener Fancy e'er could feign,
Who breeding flowers, will never breed the same;
And there shall be for thee all soft delight
That shadowy thought could win,
A bright torch, and a casement ope at night
To let the warm love in.

Keats already had the premonition that their love was fated, and indeed before the spring flowers they had planted came up he had begun spitting blood and knew that he was suffering from the fatal disease that had killed his brother. John Severn's portrait of Keats shows him sitting in his room with the fragrance of the flowery shrubbery wafting through the window. Keats House is now a museum and the garden is being restored.

Rural residences and ornamental gardening

Ornamental is the word most frequently applied to Regency gardening; it was still picturesque, that is to say 'amenable to the principles of Pictorial Art', but could tastefully accommodate the revived interest in horticulture and the linking of the house and garden. The conservatory, which was once freestanding in the garden, had become an extension of the Regency house, often being at the end of an enfilade arrangement of library, drawing room and dining room. The house and the garden were interchangeable in the provision of leisure pursuits. In 1800 W. Roberston in *Designs in Architecture* suggested combining an aviary-conservatory and a music room as 'a union of the notes of art and those of nature's choristers'.

There was direct access to the lawn from the conservatories and garden rooms with their French windows, and Regency garden designers stressed the need to 'furnish', 'dress' or ' embellish' the lawn outside. Repton thought that the gardens could be considered as 'so many different apartments' belonging to the comfort and

A Regency house with striped awnings, verandah, enfilade conservatory and 'furnished' lawn. (From Ackermann's 'Views of Country Seats', 1830. By courtesy of the Bodleian Library, Oxford.)

The approved decorative iron fence separating the 'dressed grounds' from the grazed scene as demonstrated by Repton in the Longner Hall Red Book, 1804.

Knowle Cottage, Sidmouth, Devon, about 1818, by Isaac Fidlor: a superb seaside cottage orné, built for Lord le Despencer in 1810, with Reptonian flower baskets on the lawn.

The type of 'bald and bare' landscape regarded as 'false and mistaken taste' in the Regency period.

pleasure of the house, and that 'a large lawn, like a large room when unfurnished displeases more than a small one. If only in part, or meanly furnished, we shall soon leave it in disgust, whether it be a room covered with the finest green baize, or a lawn kept with the most exquisite verdure, we look for carpets in one and flowers in the other'.

It was, by Regency times, generally accepted, as Repton set out in his Red Book proposals for Woburn Abbey in 1804, that it was 'false and mistaken taste' to site a large house 'in a naked grassfield, without any apparent line of separation between the ground exposed to cattle and the ground annexed to the house'. The Arcadian effect produced by the invisible ha-ha was to be replaced by a terrace or decorative iron fence to separate the grazed scene from the artificial 'dressed grounds'; the garden scenery would then provide a 'rich frame' to the landscape rather than become 'part of the picture'.

Knowle Cottage on a hill above Sidmouth was one of the most famous examples of a decorative Regency cottage orné, linked by a conservatory and ornamental lawn to the scenery beyond. It was open to holidaymakers and attracted thousands of visitors from miles around, for whom a special guidebook was available. Sir John Soane supervised the building of the large thatched cottage for Lord le Despencer in 1810 but it was the wealthy Thomas Fish, who bought it in 1820, who made it into a showplace. The tent-like verandah was 315 feet (96 metres) long and contained flowerstands with 3500 plants, exotic birds, globes of silver and gold fish and a telescope to observe shipping. On the lawn were ornamental shrub and flower beds edged with conch and other valuable large shells, making it, as the guidebook boasted, a most 'elegant marine villa ornée'. In 1882, some twenty years after the death of Mr Fish, his cottage orné was converted into a hotel and, more recently, it has been expanded beyond recognition into the East Devon District Council offices.

Repton's Stoneleigh Abbey, Warwickshire

The art of 'dressing' grounds pictorially was thought by Repton to have been perfected by Watteau. One place where he specifically evoked the 'richness, the amenity and the cheerfulness of his scenery' was at Stoneleigh Abbey. He had already suggested to the Prince of Wales that 'in the park scenery, we may realise the landscapes of Claude and Poussin but, in garden scenery, we delight in the rich embellishments, the blended graces of Watteau, where nature is dressed, not disfigured, by art; and where the artificial decorations of architecture and sculpture are softened down by natural accompaniments of vegetation'.

Two illustrations in the Stoneleigh Red Book of 1809, depicting 'before' and 'after' scenes by means of the usual hinged flaps, show the south front by the river Avon as Repton found it and after improvements with vases softened by flowery planting and other Watteauesque 'blended graces'. Repton had recommended reorientating the vast living accommodation so that the improved river scene could be seen from the south front, which had hitherto paid no heed of views. It was here that, in *Fragments*, Repton had indicated the horror of the 'cedar parlours' in the old Leigh mansion and he suggested in the Stoneleigh Red Book that two of the rooms should be united into one living room with four large mirrors opposite each other to repeat the enfilade in each direction.

Stoneleigh Abbey, with its outstanding Red Book, is one of the most important examples of Repton's work, undertaken at the height of his powers. Its interest is increased by Jane Austen associations.

Often Repton was called upon to redesign earlier landscaped gardens but at Stoneleigh nothing had changed for 150 years and the gardens, with a walled bowling green in front of the house, were as old-fashioned as the cedar parlours within. It gave Repton the opportunity to design a large-scale landscape adapted to Regency

Stoneleigh Abbey Red Book, 1809. 'Before' and 'after' south front scenes showing the river brought nearer the house and Watteauesque 'rich embellishments'.

Stoneleigh Abbey Red Book, 1809. Framed views of the house, weir and island from the perimeter of the grounds.

ideas of garden scenery.

'I look upon Stoneleigh Abbey as a place *sui generis* and not to be compared to any other place,' wrote Repton. Much of the landscape he designed is still to be seen today. The Avon was widened and brought nearer the house, the cattle across the river being separated by a natural barrier rather than a deceptive ha-ha; a shrubbery wilderness walk led down from the terrace to his weir, which he felt was reminiscent 'of some favourite subject of Ruysdael's pencil', especially when the effect of twilight was produced in the Red Book illustration; from a perimeter walk around the brow of a hill framed views were made of the house, weir and island in the tradition of Gilpin's picturesque 'stations'.

Reptonian ideas adapted to America

Repton's ideas were readily available through his numerous publications, which he thought would show his 'fixed principles' and establish his fame better than 'the partial and imperfect manner in which my plans have sometimes been executed'. Even in eastern Europe his illustrations served as pattern-book examples, while in North America, where the text was more easily absorbed, his principles were readily adapted to a new environment. Repton's beautiful aquatint-illustrated books were expensive, however, and aimed at wealthy landlords, but in 1840 J. C. Loudon was responsible for a great popularising of Repton's ideas when he produced a remarkably informative manual of his works at a cost of 2s 6d plain and 5s 6d coloured.

The manual consisted of *Sketches and Hints on Landscape Gardening*, originally published in 1795; *Observations on the Theory and Practice of Landscape Gardening*, 1803; *An Enquiry into the Changes of Taste in Landscape Gardening*, 1806; *Designs for the Pavillon at Brighton*, 1808, and *Fragments on the Theory and Practice of Landscape Gardening*, 1816. They included a systematic analysis, notes and a useful index by Loudon.

The year after Loudon's manual appeared, in 1841, Andrew Jackson Downing published the first major American book on rural architecture and landscape design, with the Reptonian title of *A Treatise on the Theory and Practice of Landscape Gardening, Adapted to North America*. His book, which was revised and enlarged several times, was followed the next year by *Cottage Residences; or a Series of Designs for Rural Cottages and Cottage Villas, and their Gardens and Grounds, Adapted to North America*, for which

'An Example of the Picturesque in Landscape Gardening' from A. J. Downing's 'A Treatise on the Theory and Practice of Landscape Gardening Adapted to North America', 1841.

he also had the benefit of Loudon's own *Encyclopaedia of Cottage, Farm and Villa Architecture*, 1836, and *The Suburban Gardener and Villa Companion*, 1838.

Downing had pointed out that it was highly improbable that the United States would ever achieve Great Britain's great landscaped gardens, which depended on hereditary wealth or primogeniture of large family estates. Repton and Loudon, however, had shown the way to the laying out of grounds in a picturesque style which could be adapted to a land where 'the rights of man are held to be equal'. Downing had read extensively and digested what was relevant in the writings of Price and Knight but, across the Atlantic and after an interval of over twenty years, was able to ignore the heat of the aesthetic rhetoric and see the Picturesque in perspective. As Loudon had foreseen when the Picturesque was prized apart from philosophy, there was no real Price system to follow and it was the practical 'Repton school' that held sway in landscape gardening.

Downing saw himself, like Loudon, with whom he corresponded, as an educator, and his books were directed towards the growing middle class and increasingly literate working class. He was anxious to encourage American women to undertake gardening activities and published Jane Loudon's *Gardening for Ladies* with an introduction. Like Loudon, Downing also edited the first monthly popular gardening magazine. *The Horticulturalist and Journal of Rural Art and Rural Taste*, which began circulation in 1846, offered its readers helpful hints on garden design, styles for country cottages and the latest information on new plants and technology available.

Just as Loudon in his *Gardening Magazine* took on the role of 'Conductor' to well-managed British gardens, Downing hoped through his accounts of exemplary American gardens to encourage his readers to develop a uniquely American style of 'rural art and rural taste'. For his illustrations in his books and the magazine Downing collaborated with the architect Alexander J. Davis, who had written *Rural Residences* in 1837, praising the 'picturesque Cottages and Villas of England'.

The estate for which Downing had particular esteem was Montgomery Place in the Hudson Valley, a region he regarded as highly picturesque and where in 1839 he had laid out his own Newburgh garden above the river. Downing wrote an extended article on Montgomery Place with illustrations by Davis, who designed the picturesque pavilion with its Reptonian transition from the interior of the house to the garden and landscape views. Like Repton, Downing and Davis were concerned to site garden rooms to take advantage of picturesque scenery. Downing uses Repton's term

View from Montgomery Place. (Plate 1 from 'Sketches of Montgomery Place' by A. J. Davis.)

His Majesty's Royal Lodge, Windsor. (From Ackermann's 'Views of Country Seats', 1830. By courtesy of the Bodleian Library, Oxford.)

Virginia Water, Windsor Great Park, with the Chinese junk on the lake. George Barrett, c.1765. Wyatville added a Chinese fishing temple for George IV in 1825.

'appropriate' when he refers to the picturesque siting of many of the Hudson Valley homes, where 'a residence here of but a hundred acres, so fortunately are these disposed by nature, seems to appropriate the whole scenery round, and to be a thousand in extent'.

There is a strong resemblance between the siting of the Montgomery Place pavilion and that illustrated, but not executed, in Repton's *Observations* for Plas Newydd on Anglesey, which is situated in 'dressed grounds' appropriating the picturesque views of Snowdonia across the Menai Strait. Adapted to the Hudson Valley, however, the Montgomery Place pavilion was, in Downing's words, 'a room in the open air, the greatest luxury in a warm summer; significant since it tells the story of a desiratum growing out of our climate, architecturally and fittingly supplied'.

The Prince Regent and the cottage orné

A relaxed life style away from London appealed to the Prince of Wales, especially as he had the ideal site for a scenic cottage orné in the depths of Windsor Great Park. It seems that his first encounter with the possibilities of life in a cottage orné came in 1805, through his visits to his friend Walsh Porter's newly acquired Craven Cottage by the Thames at Fulham. It had been altered by Thomas Hopper into what Croker described as 'the prettiest specimen of cottage architecture then existing'. The Gothic dining room of the so-called cottage so impressed the Prince that Hopper was given the commission of making a Gothic conservatory at Carlton House en suite with the dining room.

Windsor Castle became the asylum of King George III when the Prince became Regent in 1811. John Nash, who as Architect to the Department of Woods and Forests was responsible for the lodges in Windsor Park, was instructed by the Prince Regent to convert a lodge which had belonged to the deputy-ranger into a royal thatched sylvan cottage orné retreat. It was ornamented beyond recognition at a cost of £50,000 and much admired. A verandah, or thatched covered-way, supported by tree trunks, extended along the entire front, over which were trained honeysuckles and flowering creepers. The cottage was further expanded in the 1820s at a cost of an additional £30,000 when the great restoration of Windsor Castle by Sir Jeffrey Wyatville was undertaken and the new King George IV spent much time at his Royal Lodge cottage orné, taking charge of the operations, which were completed in 1828.

Princess Lieven describes the life style of the royal cottage orné at this time: 'We led a lazy and agreeable life there, always in the King's society. Many promenades in the forest, on the lake, sometimes dinners under tents, always music in the evening, and in everything a habit of unspoiled magnificence.' Prince Pückler-Muskau envied him such an existence, 'within the bounds of which you can live and do what you like, without privation and constraint'; all within his Great Park he could hunt, fish, ride, drive, entertain his 'cottage clique', go to the races or visit his menagerie. The German prince made light of the King's favourite giraffe going off with his umbrella.

Other members of the royal family had picturesque cottage residences with flowery Regency gardens in the park. The Princess Elizabeth, then the Dowager Duchess of Hesse-Homburg, had a cottage, according to Ackermann, which stood on a 'sweet little lawn, filled with luxuriant flowering shrubs, bounded on one side by trees and shrubs of a powerful growth, intermixed with the holly and the rose, that finely group with the sombre tints of the evergreen'. All the Windsor forest cottages enjoyed over the treetops the picturesque sight of the gigantic royal standard fluttering on the top of the round tower, which had had its original height on the mound doubled as part of Wyatville's romantic castle restoration.

Virginia Water, an artificial lake created by Thomas Sandby for George II's son, the Duke of Cumberland, was a much favoured royal place of pleasure. At the lakeside the King had a Chinese fishing temple built by Wyatville in 1825 with rows of bells, ornamental birds on the balcony roof and dragons draped round the masts. The elaborate Chinese junk, built for his great uncle, was still in use and another large boat was moored beside so that the band could play during dinner. Sometimes, for a change, the King chose to picnic in striped Turkish tents erected by the water. Virginia Water is now bereft of its exotic associations and of George IV's romantic ideas. Only the sham ruins remain in his memory. These Roman ruins were brought from Leptis Magna in Tripoli to England by a traveller in 1821 and taken to the British Museum, where they are said to have lain in the courtyard until George IV had them brought to Virginia Water and arranged by Wyatville.

John Buonarotti Papworth and garden buildings

Papworth trained under John Plaw and, like his master, frequently quotes Repton. He was also influenced by William Chambers, who had encouraged him to take up an architectural training. He was a most versatile architect and decorative artist and a great exponent of Regency technology in the use of ornamental iron. In landscape gardening he seems to have followed the ideas of William Chambers in which the garden buildings played the most significant part in the design. His two books, *Designs for Rural Residences* in 1818 and *Ornamental Gardening* in 1823, were very popular.

Papworth's designs for his decorative garden buildings were first published as aquatints in Ackermann's *Repository* in 1819 and included a bridge adapted to park scenery, a picturesque dairy 'proposed to be situated so as to form an ornament to the shrubbery', a combined ice well and tool shed, fountains, Venetian tents and highly ornamental seats as 'an elegant appendage to flower gardens'. His advice to 'persons of leisure' was that they should contemplate the activities of bees in an ornate apiary and young ladies should visit an aviary to see young birds nesting. His aviary, reminiscent of Chambers, was in the centre of 'an arcade of woodbine, roses, jessamines and other creeping and flowering shrubs' and 'embellished by flowerbeds enclosed by basket work'.

The Swiss Garden, Old Warden, Bedfordshire

The Swiss Garden, which has been restored by Bedfordshire County Council, is a unique example of the cult of the Swiss picturesque in gardening. The vogue for Alpine scenery, Swiss cottages and peasant costume seized England after the exodus to Switzerland when peace came in 1815. The best-known memorial to the Swiss cult is London's Swiss Cottage, which gives its name to a district

Apiary from J. B. Papworth, 'Hints on Ornamental Gardening', 1823.

The Swiss Garden, Old Warden: Papworth-style Swiss chalet.

Leigh Water, Leigh Park, Hampshire, with a plethora of buildings reminiscent of the imperial Chinese hunting park at Jehol, showing Corinthian bridge, fort and Chinese boathouse. J. F. Gilbert, c.1836.

Trompe l'oeil restoration of the Papworth Corinthian bridge at Leigh Park.

The Swiss Garden: thatched tree shelter in ornamental shrubberies.

and underground station. More usually such cottages were placed in romantic scenery as at Alton Towers, where a blind old Welsh harper, who had been a retainer, was retired into a Swiss cottage on the heights overlooking the grounds, or the Swiss Cottage at Endsleigh designed by Wyatville in Repton's picturesque riverside landscape.

It was P. F. Robinson who, realising the picturesque possibilities of Swiss projecting roofs, added chalets to the repertoire of pattern books. He also gave designs for Swiss bridges, mills and cowhouses made of logs and included Swiss features in his *Village Architecture*. Old Warden seems to have been the first village to receive the full picturesque treatment in mixed architectural styles as recommended by P. F. Robinson based on the principles of Price. It is undeniably in the mixed style but a few of the cottages with overhanging eaves are identifiably Swiss and the village nestles among fir trees. To put a final picturesque touch to the village, in Lord Ongley's day the women were required to wear red cloaks and tall hats.

The Swiss Garden was begun in the 1820s by Lord Ongley, whose most likely source of inspiration was Papworth's *Hints on Ornamental Gardening*. Papworth's home was nearby at Little Paxton and he was employed at several houses in the vicinity. The Papworth-style Swiss chalet, with its delicate pinecone ornamentation, is the focal point of the garden. Papworth did not specialise in Swiss architecture as Robinson did, but in his design for a Polish hut at Whiteknights, Berkshire, illustrated in his *Ornamental Gardening*, he pointed out that it resembled Swiss shelters and advocated the use of rustic unpeeled bark. Another feature from Whiteknights was the iron trellis frames covered with creeping plants forming arches over the glades. The Swiss Garden has also a fine grotto, later incorporated into a fernery, a melancholy walk to a thatched tree shelter with a marble slab on which is inscribed a sentimental poem, a garden house, a kiosk and shrubbery walks, without which no Regency garden would be complete.

Leigh Park, Hampshire

Leigh Park is a rare example of Regency ornamental gardening and has the advantage of the owner's own guidebook as documentation and many watercolours depicting it in its heyday. Sir George Staunton, who bought Leigh Park in 1820, employed no professional landscape designer but his garden reflects his own interests and expertise. Staunton spent much of his early life in China, having been a

The Swiss cult: Regency Swiss cottage built in the grounds of Brislington House private asylum for an affluent patient. T. L. S. Rowbotham, 1827. (Courtesy of City of Bristol Museum and Art Gallery.)

page on Lord Macartney's famous embassy, and when he retired to Hampshire he was recognised as the foremost cultural and political authority on China. Staunton did not choose to build himself an oriental house, as one returning nabob had done at Sezincote, but bought a modest Regency house to which he added a Gothic library to house his three thousand Chinese books.

Leigh Park's large grounds had not been worked on by an eighteenth-century improver, which gave Staunton the chance of creating a new picturesque landscape in the Repton manner. His diary refers to reading Repton's *Fragments* with its excerpts of Red Book proposals for clients. Staunton was also a keen horticulturalist, who had been encouraged by Sir Joseph Banks to collect botanical specimens when in China, and his Chinese plantings were of greater interest than the token peonies, hydrangeas and camellias planted by Repton around the Woburn Chinese dairy, as they included some new introductions and, particularly with the water plants, were used with an understanding of Chinese flower symbolism. William Kerr, the Kew botanical collector, who introduced the tiger lily, various species of peony and the so-named *Kerria japonica*, had called on Staunton in China, and later Robert Fortune sent Chinese introductions to Leigh Park.

The excavation of the lake took many years to complete and some of the ornamental buildings on it were in place before Leigh Water was flooded. One of these was a Corinthian bridge and temple across the main outlet, which Staunton acknowledged was taken from Papworth's *Ornamental Gardening*. Other ornamental lake buildings were a Turkish kiosk, a three-arched Chinese bridge and boathouse with Chinese inscriptions and an island fort displaying the imperial yellow flag of China. Such a plethora of ornamental buildings was reminiscent of the great imperial summer palace hunting park at Jehol where, with Macartney, the young George Staunton and his father had been shown 'forty or fifty different palaces or Pavilions' from the Emperor's magnificent yacht.

Leigh Park combined Picturesque landscape and horticultural interest in approved Regency style. The pleasure grounds contained Reptonian specialised flower gardens, shrubberies, glasshouses and a ferme orneé and much of this is now in the process of restoration by Hampshire County Council. Leigh Water, like George IV's Virginia Water, has looked featureless without its lively ornamental buildings but, as a start, a version of Papworth's pattern book Corinthian bridge has now been built. The restoration of Leigh Park, to a master plan, will provide an excellent example of what a Regency landscaped garden was like.

Sylva Florifera: ornamental shrubberies and specialised gardens

The Regency ornamental shrubbery was a new and distinctive addition to the pleasure ground; it followed in the line of picturesque woodland planting but added a strong floricultural element and was described, by the Brighton botanical landscape gardener Henry Phillips, as *Sylva Florifera* in a book of that title, in 1823. Phillips claimed that the ornamental shrubbery 'originated in England, and is as peculiar to the British nation as landscape-planting. Whilst other arts have derived from ancient or borrowed from modern inventions, this has indisputably sprung from the genius of our soil, and is perhaps one of the most delightful, as well as most beneficial, of all that claim the name elegant.'

In 1823 Phillips spoke as though floriferous or ornamental shrubberies were an accepted part of Regency garden design; they were used extensively in spa gardens, the early public parks and communal gardens, asylum grounds, college gardens and botanical gardens, as well as in private pleasure grounds. In Oxford, the Fellows of Worcester College, in 1817, having skilfully contrived a would-be cottage orné with curly bargeboards and trellis on the upper end of a monastic range of buildings, created a lake and a forest lawn with a perimeter Regency ornamental shrubbery in the college grounds.

The sheltered shrubbery walks broke up the spaces in public gardens, such as Sydney Gardens in Bath, giving the walkers more privacy. In 1827 all London watched while Nash and W. T. Aiton laid out St James's Park with ornamental shrubberies. They had previously experimented with such planting at the Royal Pavilion and it was here that Henry Phillips, a Brighton resident, saw their work and in 1823 drew up his first plan for laying out nearby Kemp Town with floriferous planting.

The new element in Regency-style shrubberies was their association with the theory of the Picturesque. Although William Gilpin's *Tours* had sparked off ideas on the Picturesque, it was his *Remarks on Forest Scenery (Relative Chiefly to Picturesque Beauty)*, published in 1791, which had most influence on landscape gardening. This was written when he settled in a living in the New Forest and exchanged the delights of the picturesque observation of lakes and mountains for forest scenery. In his book Gilpin maintained that landscape gardeners would do well to study the planting in the

Worcester College, Oxford: the college garden was given a picturesque layout in the 1820s with lake and ornamental shrubberies; from the left the framed views are of the Provost's lodgings, the library and the orné effect of the gabled end of the monastic range.

New Forest, 'finer than any garden you ever saw', he wrote to his friend and ally William Mason, author of *The English Garden*, soon after he had arrived in Hampshire in 1777. Mason, who laid out Lord Harcourt's flower garden at Nuneham, was the first landscape gardener to take up Gilpin's 'forest scenery' ideas and in the fourth book of *The English Garden*, published in 1782, he wrote:

> His taste will best conceive
> The new arrangement, whose free footsteps, us'd
> To forest haunts, have pierc'd their opening dells,
> Where frequent tufts of sweetbriar, box, or thorn,
> Steal on the greensward, but admit fair space
> For many a mossy maze to wind between.

The 'new arrangement' was the result of Gilpin's analysis of the planting of the wood pasture or New Forest 'lawndes', browsed by forest animals into a fine turf, which were 'adorned with islands or peninsulas of forest scenery shooting into them'. Gilpin had suggested that it was possible to 'apply to artificial landscape those observations which occur in natural for the source of beauty is the same in both'. The 'lawns of Hagley' were but 'paltry imitations'.

Price in his *Essay on the Picturesque* took up Gilpin's idea of studying the 'forest lawn' and the 'forest thicket', which had 'a great advantage in point of variety, and playfulness of outline'. William Sawrey Gilpin, Gilpin's nephew and a disciple of Price, wrote in his *Practical Hints on Landscape Gardening* in 1832 that 'good hints' for planting 'could be found on any common, where furze, broom etc, furnish varieties of form and groupings'.

  A. J. Downing contrasted this type of picturesque shrubbery with the 'arabesque' or beautiful grouping of shrubs, which had flourished in the earlier perimeter shrubbery walks inspired by Hogarth's 'line of beauty'. In the eighteenth century trees, shrubs and flowers were usually separate components in the landscaped garden. Trees were planted in avenues, clumps and belts or singly on lawns and flowers held sway in flower gardens. Gilpin's *Remarks on Forest Scenery* showed how in natural scenes shrubs and flowers grew in harmony and connected the landscape. 'Besides the forest trees, in which the dignity of woodland scenery consists, it is inriched by a variety of humble plants, which filling up the interstices, mass and connect the whole.'

A New Forest lawn 'adorned with islands and peninsulas of forest scenery shooting into them'.

Gilpin extols the beauty of holly and hawthorn mixed with oak and continues: 'nor are shrubs alone useful in harmonizing the forest, the larger kinds of weeds, and wild flowers have their effect in filling up the smaller vacancies near the ground; and add to the richness of the whole.' J. C. Loudon, in his *Observations on the Formation and Management of Useful and Ornamental Plantations* in 1804, claimed that this forest lawn planting was his own idea and, although this was not strictly true, it shows that, when he wrote, the ornamental shrubbery was a rarity. He does give a very good description of what Regency gardening set out to achieve:

'...such a variety of trees, shrubs, flowers, etc, as that a number of each will be in perfection every month of the year, particularly in the summer season. They should be placed in irregular groups and thickets, of different sizes, gliding into one another on smooth lawn, beautifully varied, broken into small scenes by trees and shrubs of the most elegant sorts. Throughout the whole, smooth gravel walks should wind in a graceful, easy manner.'

In 1807, after Loudon had worked at Ditchley Park on these Gilpin-inspired ideas, he wrote: 'everyone must allow it to be interesting to see exotic trees, shrubs and flowers grouped and scattered over lawns in the same way that thorns, oaks, hazels and weeds are in our forests.' It was the natural grouping of the brakes and tufts on the forest lawns, the intermixing of plants and not the actual weeds which were to be copied, of course. When the gardener imitated such forest lawns the actual content of the shrubbery would be native or exotic plants, then arriving in increasing numbers, and ordered from the nurseryman's catalogue.

Henry Phillips's *Sylva Florifera* set out to show how these floriferous shrubberies should be planted and the wealth of shrubs and herbaceous plants available to the Regency gardener. The shrubs, mainly evergreen, were to be planted first, with great attention to be paid to the shades of green; into the spaces were recessed flowers such as hollyhocks, martagon lilies, peonies, foxgloves, day lilies, sunflowers and Michaelmas daisies. Up the bare trunks of trees and woody shrubs were grown passion flowers, clematis, everlasting peas, trailing arbutus, trumpet flowers, flaming nasturtium, jasmine and honeysuckles. The shrubs and small trees in a shrubbery walk, arranged with due regard to seasonal flowering, included acacia, dogwood, viburnum, the Judas tree, euonymus, dwarf almonds, guelder-rose, lilac, philadelphus, Chinese privet, phillyrea, kalmia, brooms, sumach, gorse and laurel, and one of the most important components was sweetbriars and Scotch roses. The new China roses were also highly recommended.

Phillips had painterly ideas on aerial perspective in planting and recommended placing grey or bluish leaved plants beyond or between yellow or bright green shrubs; and that 'the light and elegant acacia has a more beautiful effect when its branches float over the firm and dark holly or bay tree'; also broom should be planted to 'peep over the sombre evergreens like the rays of the sun' and the guelder-rose should appear as if 'escaping from the dark bosom of evergreens'.

Crescent Garden, Alverstoke, Gosport

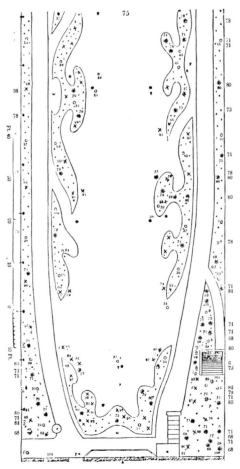

The most detailed information on the planting of a Regency ornamental shrubbery is given by J. C. Loudon in *The Suburban Gardener and Villa Companion*, where a plan is followed by a key to the low growing flowering trees, roses and shrubs chosen; only the herbaceous plants to be recessed into the shrubbery are missing, but these are to be chosen by the lady of the house herself. Loudon also gives hints on management with a warning about removal of large trees. When the ornamental shrubbery was not managed properly it turned into a dull mass of the dominant evergreens, which is why it fell out of favour. In some cases the spire tree in the shrub bed was allowed

Loudon's plan of a small garden for a client who wanted a 'Sylva Florifera' picturesque layout, from 'The Suburban Gardener and Villa Companion', 1838.

to grow so tall that nothing grew under it.

Loudon's plan is being carefully followed by the Friends of the newly created Crescent Garden at Alverstoke. These are public gardens for a crescent of terraced houses, designed by Thomas Ellis Owen in 1828 as part of an ambitious, but abortive, project to create a new Regency seaside spa. Jane Austen's sailor brother, Charles, lived at Number 2. The gardens, which had originally had a neo-classical bath-house in the centre and a shrubbery walk with peephole scenes of the Isle of Wight, had become very neglected when the Friends group was founded by Mrs Wendy Osborne, the wife of a retired naval officer, who lives in the Crescent.

The residents, working with an enlightened borough council, have taken the greatest trouble to find what was still hidden in the jungle and, having decided on authentic Regency planting, have spared no pains in finding nurseries to supply the right period plants. The railings have been restored, grant-aided by English Heritage, and seats and flowerstands have been copied from engravings, the latter to resemble that seen in Repton's own garden.

The flower garden

Eighteenth-century landscaping for the most part banished flowers to the walled kitchen garden, although there were always keen naturalists and gardeners, such as Gilbert White of Selborne, who paid great attention to floriculture. There were also Thomas Wright inspired rosaries and tufts or cabinets of flowers in secluded glades in rococo gardens and Dickie Bateman's garden at Old Windsor was praised by Walpole as 'a kingdom of flowers'. Southcote's Woburn ferme ornée was famous for its perimeter flowery hedges 'enriched with woodbine, jessamine and every odoriferous plant whose tendrils will entwine with the thicket'.

The Nuneham flower garden

The greatest influence on the flower garden as an integral part of Regency landscape design, however, was Earl Harcourt's famous flower garden at Nuneham Courtenay, designed in 1772 by the poet-gardener William Mason. Laid out with 'Poet's feeling and Painter's eye', his informal flower garden was acclaimed as a revolution in taste and sentiment. Everybody raved about it – the royal family, Walpole, Reynolds, who found it 'irresistible', John Wesley and Mrs Siddons, who found it did her more good than any church service; poems extolled it and it was made famous by Paul Sandby's paintings. The Nuneham engravings in the *Copperplate Magazine* in 1778 showed the picturesque possibility of a landscape with flowers,

Sydney Gardens in Bath. Aquatint by G. Wise showing the curving canal towpath with the Chinese-style bridge crossing the Regency gardens. (Courtesy of Bath Reference Library.)

The Crescent Garden, Alverstoke: a Regency garden being laid out on the principles of the Loudon layout.

Nuneham Courtenay, Oxfordshire: view of Lord Harcourt's Flower Garden. (Engraved by W. Watts after Paul Sandby, 1777.)

and real gardeners are depicted and not bogus shepherds as figures in the landscape.

The cult of flowers and sensibility went hand in hand in Mason's garden. Lord Harcourt greatly admired Rousseau, and his garden was based on Julie's garden in *La Nouvelle Heloise*, where Nature was to inspire feelings of virtue as well as of pleasure. To make sure that the soul was raised to virtue in Nuneham's Elysée, sentimental inscriptions and statues to men of virtue, including Rousseau, and memorials to dead friends who 'living lov'd the haunts' were placed in the shrubbery. The flower garden changed in character after the association of Mason and Lord Harcourt with Gilpin, who had less sentimental and more practical ideas on Nature than Rousseau.

The plan of 1785 shows the 'new arrangement' Mason referred to in *The English Garden* and which he had learned from Gilpin's New Forest scenery. No plan exists which shows the previous layout of the garden Sandby painted, where the flowerbeds are seen to be edged formally with box. In the new plan the graduated clumps, some of flowers and some of shrubs, glide in a forest lawn appearance; the clumps on each side of the temple are flowers backed by shrubs. In 1794 the Earl made another 'material alteration' to

The watercolour Repton pasted in the Nuneham guidebook, written by Lord Harcourt and given to him on his visit; it shows the urn dedicated to Viscountess Palmerston in the flower garden with the sentimental inscription by Whitehead: 'O! if kind pity steal on virtue's eye/Check not the tear, nor stop the useful sigh.'

Nuneham plan of 1785 showing William Mason's forest lawn arrangement. (PRO Work 38/349.)

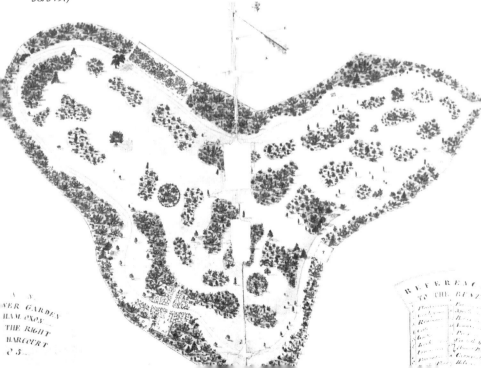

Repton flowerstands as used in his own Hare Street garden and copied in the Crescent Garden.

Ashridge, Hertfordshire: Repton's circular rosarium, 1814, the form of which remains.

Hluboka Castle, Moravia, Czech Republic, in the Scots baronial style.

been reading Scott in bed had her own ancient Hluboka Castle knocked down, to be replaced by a Scots baronial Tully Veolan.

As Scott demonstrated at his own Abbotsford, where in 1816 he laid out a garden with a screen copied from Melrose Abbey, architectural ornaments from the Old Cross in Edinburgh and trellis work, naked lawns were not in keeping with baronial buildings. Scott upheld the 'propriety of retaining every shred connected with history or antiquity' and Southey maintained that historical associations in gardens were 'a matter of feeling, which is a better thing than taste'. Sir John Soane produced accompanying diagrams of formal historic gardens when he gave lectures on architecture after 1814. Loudon gave an account of the formal national styles in his *Encyclopaedia of Gardening* in 1822.

Drummond Castle, Perthshire

The home of the Drummonds, ardent royalists, who had been closely in contact with the exiled Jacobite court, was the ideal place for romantic revival. It was not until 1785 that the Drummond family regained their estate after their involvement in the 1745 rising and then fashionably naturalised their parkland.

In 1820 romantic revivalism came to Drummond Castle, oddly enough from the south, when Lewis Kennedy, who had laid out the formal garden at Chiswick in front of the conservatory, became factor of the Drummond estates. He almost certainly created the remarkable parterre flower garden, which in a modified form exists today. The dominant feature is the St Andrew's cross radiating from the existing Renaissance obelisk sundial; the base is set in a

Specialised garden at Mount Edgcumbe, Cornwall: the French garden c.1803.

Bessborough, with four supporting figures resembling mermaids, composed of white stone and of Italian workmanship. Mount Edgcumbe provides a rare example of this Regency arrangement of specialised gardens linked by ornamental shrubberies.

Romantic revivalism

Walter Scott invented a new kind of national history. Inspired by his border minstrelsy and historic novels, a Regency observer could view, through romantic spectacles, the stirring events of the past without prejudice or partisanship. The Prince Regent, who doted on the novels, lost no time in honouring his ancestors, to the consternation of some Whigs, and, under Scott, arranged for the Stuart papers to be edited. After his accession, Scott was one of the first knights to be created, the King refusing to let him kneel for the ceremony. In 1822 Sir Walter stage-managed the royal visit to Edinburgh and resuscitated the ancient traditions of the Scottish monarchy. The King, resplendent in his Stuart kilt and tartan, was delighted by Scott's theatrical pageantry, no reigning sovereign having set foot on Scottish soil since Charles II.

Walter Scott revitalised Gothic architecture when his novels appeared in rapid succession. His castles, associated with stirring historical scenes, fed the imagination of an age already visually prepared for irregular architecture by Gilpin, Knight and Price. Scots baronial mansions, in imitation of Tully Veolan in *Waverley*, with its angle turrets, crow-stepped gables, battlements and steep roofs, sprang up all over Britain. Even as far afield as Moravia, a lady who had the wider landscape, like Julie's Elysée, for Johnes's daughter, Mariamne, it was the type of flower garden Mason advocated for his heroine, Nerina, in Book IV.

> Why, on these forest features all intent,
> Forbears my friend some scene distinct to give
> To Flora and her fragrance?

Mrs Johnes also had her flower garden, an American garden with peaty soil, on the valley bottom. Her delicate daughter, Mariamne, who was a keen botanist, had a steeply sloping garden, divided into five distinct areas, for different kinds of plants, particularly alpines, first planted in 1795.

Specialised gardens

Specialised gardens were a Repton introduction, which he first mentioned in *Observations* in 1803. He advocated ancient gardens, American gardens with 'beds of bog earth' and 'different characters of taste in gardening'. In 1813 he was to propose at Ashridge fifteen such gardens, including a rosarium and a 'monk's garden' with a holy well, to offset Wyatt's abbey architecture. These 'episodes' had to be well insulated and at Woburn, where there was a Chinese and a children's garden with individual named bowers, Repton insisted on *English Garden* type shrubbery walks connecting the whole, 'decently chaperoned by English shrubberies' as Frank Clark commented.

Mount Edgcumbe, Cornwall

The best example of Reptonian specialised gardens can be seen at Mount Edgcumbe. They were made by the second Earl Mount Edgcumbe and his wife and taken out of the large Mason-type flower garden which had been created by the first Earl in the early 1780s just after the publication of Mason's Book IV of *The English Garden*, which contains instructions for making flower gardens. The Mount Edgcumbes were close friends of his patron, Lord Harcourt, and Mason visited them in 1783. The special character gardens, made in 1803, were chaperoned from each other by ornamental shrubberies.

The French garden was laid out as a little square enclosure bounded by a high hedge of evergreen oak and bay with a formal parterre surrounded by trellis arcades and a central shell fountain. A mirror backing an antique statue of Meleager in an octagonal room at the end of the garden reflects the parterre. When the Countess, who had created the garden, died in 1806 an urn was placed in the spot she loved. The layout of the Italian garden was determined by an existing orangery, and a handsome diagonal stairway with statues was made opposite. On the central axis was a fountain, the gift of Lord

Mount Edgcumbe, the Italian garden by Nicholas Condy. The garden was created around an existing orangery c.1803. (Courtesy of the Western Morning News Co Ltd.)

the flower garden, which probably introduced the shrubbery mingled with flowers which became increasingly popular as *sylva florifera* in Regency gardens.

Mason's flower garden was widely copied. At Stoke Park, near Windsor, Loudon referred to the flower garden, with its busts and statues, as 'of the Mason School of Design'. Queen Charlotte called on Mason to advise on a new flower garden for Frogmore in 1791, saying to Lord Harcourt: 'How much must not Mr Mason feel when he sees his own taste not only answer to the owner, but doing justice to by the generality of people.' Mason was unwell at the time and sent his picturesque curate, Christopher Alderson, to Frogmore as his understudy. Repton visited Lord Harcourt in 1798 and admired the flower garden, which he illustrated in Peacock's *Repository*. Although he used the gliding forest lawn shrub planting in his own designs, Repton was never happy with the sentimental side of Nuneham.

Mariamne's garden, Hafod

Mason's book was very influential and Thomas Johnes declared that he had laid out Hafod with '*The English Garden* in hand'. Set in

Drummond Castle: Romantic revival flower garden with Drummond heraldic devices.

Audley End, Essex: reinstated Regency flower parterre backed by ornamental shrubberies by William Sawrey Gilpin, 1832.

mosaic of pebbles forming black and white wavy bands, taken from the Drummond heraldic devices. Large orders of plants were sent up from the Lee and Kennedy nurseries in Hammersmith.

Audley End, Essex

Audley End still stood in the middle of a pastoral landscape when the third Baron Braybrooke embarked on a romantic revival of the interior of his Jacobean house in 1825. William Sawrey Gilpin was called in to provide a contemporary garden and he must have been delighted to find an owner of a 'manorial building' who wanted to bring back what his mentor Uvedale Price had called 'the rich formality of the old school'.

Gilpin was not instructed to make a true restoration of a parterre with intricate patterns of box tracery on coloured gravels but one with a design of flowers then available, which, as was usual with Regency parterres, ensured that on the ground the planting seemed only semi-formal; from the windows of the new Jacobean rooms, however, the parterre appeared formally authentic. Following archaeology and detailed research English Heritage has carried out a most commendable restoration of the parterre and is planning to restore the adjoining ornamental shrubberies which formed an integral part of the design.

Windsor Castle, Berkshire

Windsor, which became George IV's passion, is the greatest of the romantically restored castles; 'the most splendid of all the royal residences occupied by any European prince', enthused Pückler-Muskau. George IV supervised Wyatville's work from Windsor Lodge and at a great Christmas house-warming in 1828 took possession of his new Windsor Castle, two years before he died. The principal change was the conversion of the east front into private apartments, leaving the old royal suites to the north to serve as state apartments with a new grand corridor 550 feet (168 metres) long for displaying his royal collections.

The east front commanded the noblest baroque vista in Britain, the 3 mile (5 km) drive from the castle, with elms planted in 1680. George IV cleared an obstructing building and terminated the avenue with a great equestrian statue to his father. Charles II's old bowling green under the new royal apartments was replaced by the east terrace parterre garden, laid out by Aiton, the royal gardener. George IV positioned the marble vases and statues in it himself. As was to be expected, George IV's Windsor Castle and its landscape was the most spectacular example of romantic historicism.

The Royal Pavilion and the cult of the exotic

The fantastic Royal Pavilion still astounds visitors as it was intended to do when its domes and minarets first began to rise up by the seaside at Brighton in 1818. Exoticism and the Byronic longing for remote untrodden ways fired the Prince's imagination as much as Walter Scott inspired the images and background of his native Stuart 'ancestral voices'. Not that the Prince had any opportunity, or indeed inclination, to become an unconstitutional monarch, but he savoured the theatrical splendour of despotism. The name of the Great Moghul had for long conjured up visions of dazzling palaces and pleasure domes but few Europeans had ever seen them. In 1803, when the British at last occupied Delhi, the dream became a reality as Moghul monuments could be explored

The Prince had remembered, from his childhood at Kew, Muntz's Alhambra in the gardens, but this was unauthentically conjured up 'in the old Moorish Taste'. The first essay for the Prince in genuine Indian was the spectacular royal stables and riding school erected on the northern side of the grounds of the Brighton marine pavilion in 1803 by William Porden. It was not long, however, before the Prince protested that his horses, placed in forty-four stalls in a circle under the dome with a central watering fountain, were housed more splendidly than he was himself.

The marine pavilion the Prince had lived in since 1787, after his clandestine marriage to Mrs Fitzherbert, was still modest enough, adapted by Henry Holland from a farmhouse with bays and projecting wings and chinoiserie interiors. It was Repton who gave substance to the royal thoughts of converting it into an exotic Moghul seaside fantasy to outshine the splendid stables. Samuel Rogers had commented that Porden's stables looked 'like one of those Indian mausoleums in Daniell's Views' and it was to Thomas Daniell and his *Oriental Scenery* that Repton turned for inspiration when he was summoned to Brighton in 1805 for advice on creating a Moghul palace which would astonish the Prince's friends.

Thomas Daniell and his nephew William gave a new dimension to Regency architecture by their depiction of oriental buildings set in oriental scenery. They made a vast stock of drawings of Hindu temples, Moghul mosques, tombs and palaces which were not just picturesque impressions but accurately delineated by camera obscura. Their work showed architects and designers the rich possibilities of Indian architecture and was as important as the *Antiquities of Athens* had

'Hindoo Temple' from Thomas and William Daniell's 'Oriental Scenery', the inspiration for Indian architecture.

Valleyfield, Fife, c.1800, where Repton 'dared to make a perfectly strait gravel path'; from 'Observations on the Theory and Practice of Landscape Gardening', 1803.

The west corridor from Repton's 'Designs for the Pavillon at Brighton': a long continuous conservatory corridor would have linked the Pavilion to the dome and the garden buildings. Detail from Nash's 'Views' showing the western lawn approach to Brighton Pavilion with forest lawn planting, which contrasts with Repton's proposed flower baskets and containers as embellished garden scenery.

been to eighteenth-century classicism. The Daniells' published aquatints had the advantage over Stuart's engravings of appearing in colourful splendour.

Sezincote, Gloucestershire

The first piece of lived-in Hindu architecture to be built in England, at a time when Porden's royal stables were going up, was at Sezincote in Gloucestershire. It was built for Charles Cockerell, a retired nabob from the East India Company, by his brother, the architect Samuel Pepys Cockerell, and the Prince of Wales was one of its earliest visitors. He was clearly impressed by its green onion dome, chujjahs, chattris and purdah windows. It was a lively trio who were infusing the oriental magic into Sezincote: Samuel Pepys Cockerell, Humphry Repton and Thomas Daniell.

It was in the Red Book of *Designs for the Pavillon at Brighton*, published in 1808, that Repton spoke of his association with Thomas Daniell and his influence on his subsequent ideas on landscape gardening. He tells of his excitement as 'a new field opened itself' through Daniell's 'new sources of beauty and variety'. Although Samuel Pepys Cockerell was the architect of Sezincote, Repton, with his sons, helped the Cockerells choose the most picturesque elements of 'Hindoo architecture' to reproduce from Daniell's drawings. Repton recognised that the new cast iron could be 'peculiarly adapted to some light parts of the Indian style'. His advice would have been particularly valued in the setting of the Indian garden buildings, which Daniell designed himself.

At the head of the valley is the lotus-shaped temple pool, where the Hindu sun goddess Souriya presides in her shrine. On either side are rockwork caves with a larger grotto among the trees. A stream flows down the valley, beneath a stone bridge supported by Hindu columns, and below the bridge is the Serpent Pool, so-called because the water circulates round a little island on which is a dead tree trunk with a three-headed snake coiling up it; it is actually a water pipe conducting water to the snake's fangs, where it spurts out in triplicate, a symbol of regeneration.

The spirit of India, complete with symbolical snakes, stone sacred bulls and lotus buds, is all pervasive as the visitor walks under the bridge on stepping stones to gaze at the pool. In 1817 John Martin was commissioned to make views of Sezincote, one of which shows the flower garden Repton advocated as the appropriate accompaniment to the south front of the house with its curving conservatory. This has now been replaced by a narrow rectangular canal and cypresses. The temple pool, however, still looks the same as in the Martin drawing

Sezincote, Gloucestershire: the Temple Pool, with the north side of the house, by John Martin, 1817. (Photograph from Courtauld Institute of Art.)

and the first objects to be seen on the walk to the house are Daniell's Brahminy bulls, which he insisted must be sited on the bridge as that was where 'the Artist of the Gods of the Hindoos' would have placed them.

Repton and the Brighton Pavilion

The Prince of Wales had originally seemed happy enough with the architectural aspects of his marine pavilion. In 1801 P. F. Robinson had given the Holland classical front facing the sea picturesque additions of green-painted tent-shaped metal canopies to the balconies, which soon became delightful features of seaside Regency houses. In 1802 a Chinese gallery was formed to take some Chinese wallpapers the Prince had been given and gradually the Chinese manner in decoration and furniture prevailed. Designs were also made, but not executed, for a Chinese-fronted exterior, at the same time as the Porden stables were being built.

The Moghul stables then appeared as a vast Kew-like garden building dominating the scene and Repton was summoned to advise the Prince of Wales on a new layout after more land had been acquired and East Street, which ran through the grounds, closed. Repton had already worked at Brighton in a minor capacity in altering surface levels some

Nash built castellated East Cowes Castle on the Isle of Wight for himself in 1798. Aiton later sent exotic plants from Kew for the garden.
Brighton Pavilion: restoration of the western lawn showing Porden's dome (now a theatre) in the background.

years before and was clearly delighted to receive the new summons from the Pavilion on 17th November 1805. He recalled, in his *Memoir*, the letter and his immediate response:

'"Sir, I have received the Prince of Wales' commands to say His Royal Highness will be glad to have your opinion upon the Gardens of the Pavilion, as soon as you can conveniently come" – I turned my horse's head round and set off immediately to answer this letter in person. I announced my arrival at Brighton, but the Prince did not fix a time for seeing me until the 24th – I was prepared to take notice of the first words he should speak, and I had not been ten minutes alone in the room when he entered and with all that particular grace which no one can conceive who has not seen it, he said "I am sorry to have kept you waiting Mr Repton – but I wished to be perfectly at liberty to talk to you".'

Although Repton was consulted in his capacity as landscape gardener, the Prince was well aware that Repton and Nash saw buildings and landscape as 'a picturesque whole' and it is clear that Repton's 'on-the-spot' discussions went beyond proposals for garden scenery and involved plans for an Indian palace and gardens. Repton thought Chinese architecture would be 'too light and trifling' for the exterior and that instead of treating Porden's stable dome as a garden building, it should serve as a complement to a new spectacular Indian building. The Prince was obviously receptive and Repton wrote later of 'the elegance and facility of the Prince's own invention' in the matter. Repton had always hoped for a royal commission and to succeed as architect as well as landscape gardener, and now, with the help of his two architect sons, it seemed as if his dream would come true.

The Red Book for the Royal Pavilion showing the proposed Indian palace and pleasure grounds was presented to the Prince of Wales in 1806 and the Prince declared himself delighted with it. 'Mr Repton,' he said, 'I consider the whole of this work as perfect and will have every part of it carried into immediate execution, not a tittle shall be altered – even you yourself shall not attempt any improvement.' However, there was an important factor to be considered, which Repton recalled in his *Memoir*. The Prince's privy purse was long since overspent but Repton was more inclined to blame Mrs Fitzherbert's influence for the failure of his cherished scheme, accusing her of having 'eyes which shone to be admired, rather than to admire anything'. She showed no interest in Repton's Red Book and the only remark she made was 'And pray what is all this to cost?'

Repton had made it clear in his Red Book that oriental palaces did not spring up out of the lawn, banishing 'all the gay accompaniments of a garden', in the manner of a landscaped park, as Lapidge, Brown's assistant, had previously treated Holland's marine villa. As Daniell had shown in his *Oriental Scenery*, the palaces of great rulers were surrounded by gardens, full of flowers and buildings for pleasure. Repton would give his pleasure-loving Prince 'a true garden' with 'rich embellishments'.

The Prince, who had accompanied Repton when he surveyed the grounds in 1805, 'talked as if he had never thought of any subject than gardens, Parks and landscapes', according to Repton. The Prince had told him that he had been much pleased to note that he had 'dared to make a perfectly strait gravel walk'. This was probably Repton's illustration for Valleyfield, 'a design for a rectilinear pleasure garden' in *Observations*, and Repton did not hesitate to suggest a square, rose-bordered pool for the Pavilion, like a lakeside garden in Kashmir, where musicians could play on a platform. A pheasantry with flower-enwreathed columns and an aviary were both modelled on drawings from *Oriental Scenery*.

A 'Chinese garden', so marked on Repton's plan showing the east lawn, with a profusion of wicker flower baskets, could be stepped into from the rooms decorated with Chinese wallpapers. This type of Chinese garden was not in the spirit of the great Jehol hunting park as would be created by Staunton at Leigh Park, but rather a Canton courtyard garden crowded with flowers in containers. The perfume of flowers would float in through the windows to the Prince's apartments and a long continuous flower-filled conservatory corridor, a 'perpetual garden' with a regular succession of plants, would link the Pavilion, stables and garden buildings for use in inclement weather.

Although nothing came of Repton's proposals for the Prince of Wales, he was allowed to publish the Red Book in 1808 as *Designs for the Pavillon at Brighton*, which was much acclaimed and included in Loudon's manual of Repton's works of 1840. Repton had been determined to show the Prince how much could be achieved in the way of garden art in a small space and that 'instead of regretting we had only 5 acres, we could not require more to make these gardens perfect of their kind'. Henceforth Repton's ideas would concentrate on garden scenery and 'blended graces of Watteau' rather than wider landscaping. Flora, for long banished to distant enclosures, held her own, in the Frontispiece, above the once unthinkable inscription that 'Gardens are Works of Art rather than Nature'.

Repton acknowledged this change of heart came from his experience of working with Thomas Daniell and his realisation that 'we were on the eve of some great change in landscape gardening' as a result of oriental influence. Henceforth ornamental flower gardens, as part of the interaction of the house and garden, became part of Repton's

recommended improvements. Urns 'softened by vegetation', flower-wreathed columns and the so-called Chinese flower baskets with their wicker edgings seen in the Brighton *Designs* became very popular. The last have more recently been copied by Geoffrey Jellicoe at Little Horsted, Sussex.

Nash and the Prince Regent's Pavilion

The Prince was inaugurated as Regent in 1811 and characteristically, to Queen Charlotte's chagrin, held a magnificent fête, ostensibly in celebration of his father's birthday. The event was stage-managed by Nash at Carlton House, with covered walks in the garden built as promenades and supper galleries in the manner of Vauxhall pleasure gardens. Nash was Architect of the Department of Woods and Forests and the Regent now had official access to his talents, not only through his plan for Regent's Park in 1811 but with the royal 'thatched palace' in Windsor Park in 1813, for which Nash hoped to reduce the Prince's privy purse expenditure by drawing on the 'lop and top of the Forest', which came under the jurisdiction of his Department.

It was obvious that the Prince would call on Nash's ingenuity when he finally decided what he wanted for his fantasy Pavilion at Brighton, which even by the Prince's cavalier reckoning would be costly. His new flamboyant architect was better able to cater for the increased splendour of the royal life style than Repton had been, particularly as Mrs Fitzherbert, and her sobering influence, had now left the scene. Nash had been virtually a courtier at Carlton House and it was rumoured that he married a young woman reputed to be the Prince's mistress more to oblige his royal master than to please himself. Nash's *pièce de resistance* at Carlton House had been the fête in honour of Wellington in 1814, for which he had built a great twelve-sided, tent-roofed ballroom, 120 feet (36.5 metres) in diameter, in the middle of which was a floral temple concealing two orchestras. It was later transferred to Woolwich Arsenal.

With Waterloo fought and won, the Prince Regent could turn his attention to a seaside extravaganza with a clear conscience. Nash had been lent Daniell's *Oriental Scenery* from the royal library and had the advantage of knowing Repton's *Designs for the Pavillon at Brighton*, published in 1808. To Repton's bitter disappointment, in spite of the Prince's enthusiastic affirmation that his designs represented the definitive ideas for the Pavilion and its gardens, he had never bothered to reclaim the manuscript Red Book from the publisher. Nash's unpublished preface to his own *Views of the Royal Pavilion, Brighton* said that the primary purpose of the Prince and his architect was that the desired Indian effect should be 'not pedantic but picturesque'. Porden's dome and Repton's ideas for the Pavilion, taken from the camera-obscura accurate illustrations in *Oriental Scenery*, were seen as lacking in imagination. Nash's 'turban domes and pinnacles' and tent-like structures, aimed at 'glittering and picturesque effect', were more in tune with the mood of 1816, the year that 'Kubla Khan', with its romantic vision of pleasure domes, was published.

At Xanadu did Kubla Khan
A stately pleasure dome decree
Where Alph, the sacred river, ran
Through caverns measureless to man
Down to a sunless sea.

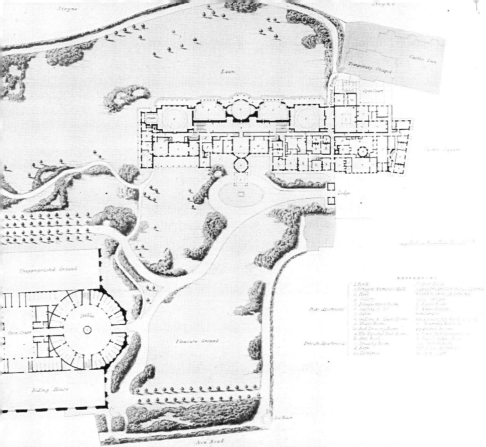

Nash's plan of the Pavilion from 'Views' showing the layout of ornamental shrubberies in the grounds, now being restored. The initiative for the restoration came from Mr John McCarthy, founder of the Sussex Historic Gardens Restoration Society in 1983.

Xanadu, Kubla Khan and Alph, like the Arabian Nights, were of a splendid hybrid culture, as were the Prince's new fanciful ideas for the Brighton Pavilion; they seemed to embody a celebration of victory over Napoleon, in which the Prince was sure he had played a significant part, as seen through Coleridge's opium dreams. When things looked difficult, Queen Charlotte, the year before she died, contributed £50,000 from her own purse to her son's extravaganza.

Instead of erecting temporary marquees, supper boxes and dancing pavilions for fêtes, as at Carlton House, Nash's two great rooms, the music room and the banqueting hall, with their gorgeous decorations, including spectacular chandeliers, were added to the original marine villa structure and provided the Prince Regent with all he needed for a theatrical setting for the voluptuous life style much caricatured by the press. In the words of Princess Lieven: 'I do not believe that since the days of Heliogabalus there has been such magnificence and luxury. One spends the evening half-lying on cushions; the lights are dazzling; there are perfumes, music, liqueurs.'

The Pavilion gardens: Nash and Aiton

There was considerably less emphasis on the gardens in Nash's scheme than there had been in Repton's *Designs for the Pavillon at Brighton*, not only because Nash was primarily an architect, but because the Prince Regent, who was growing progressively more obese and gout-ridden, was less interested in walking and appearing in a spot so open to the public gaze. He preferred his musicians inside the Pavilion rather than by the open flower-bordered square pool Repton had suggested and finally, instead of the covered walk Repton would have provided for him to the stables, an underground passage was built from the Pavilion for the royal inspection of the horses. The Prince, who succeeded to the throne in 1820, when the gardens were still immature, visited Brighton only once between 1825 and his death in 1830, preferring his Windsor Royal Lodge for relaxation and a phaeton ride across the park to Virginia Water for exercise.

Instead of Repton's 'true garden' to walk in, with 'rich embellishments' to view, all that had been required was a picturesque setting for Nash's Pavilion, which would offset the domes and minarets and frame a varying succession of features of the intriguing skyline from the carriage drive. Whereas Repton was anxious to separate the concept of the garden and the park, Nash, who had given the landscape park a new lease of life in his metropolitan improvements, used the same ideas for Brighton; this was 'forest lawn' scenery based on the ideas of Gilpin, Mason, Price and Loudon such as he first used in Regent's Park and subsequently as 'ornamental shrubberies' for St James's Park.

Nash was no horticulturalist, however, and could not have carried out his successful landscape gardening, the principles of which he had learned from working with Repton, if it had not been for the assistance of William Townsend Aiton, the royal gardener and a founder of the Royal Horticultural Society in 1805; indeed many people attributed the Brighton gardens entirely to him. Loudon's obituary of W. T. Aiton on 24th May 1850 reads: 'on the accession of King George IV Mr Aiton was not only continued in all his appointments, but received the Royal command to make the new garden at the Pavilion but also that of Buckingham Palace.'

Certainly Aiton's plan for Buckingham Palace closely resembles the layouts of Nash's St James's Park and the Brighton Pavilion and from other evidence it seems that Nash and Aiton worked as a team on royal commissions, with Aiton supplying the horticultural expertise. Aiton, who was virtually in charge of the Kew collections, even had plants sent from Kew to Nash, including *Nandinia domestica, Banksia latifolia, Bignonia capensis* and *Kennedia rubicunda*, for his own East Cowes Castle garden.

New exotic plants were constantly arriving in Britain at this time from the Cape, Australasia and China. The perfumed riches of Cathay, peonies, roses and chrysanthemums, hitherto seen only on the wallpapers, could now bloom at Brighton. Aiton briefed the plant-hunter William Kerr to go out to Canton, and his introductions, including *Kerria japonica* and the tiger lily, were propagated by Aiton at Kew and doubtless found their way into Nash's ornamental shrubberies.

The restoration of the grounds of the Brighton Pavilion

Queen Victoria found the lack of privacy at the Brighton Pavilion unbearable. When her new seaside residence at Osborne was completed, she had the Pavilion stripped and in 1850 it became the property of the town: new paths were laid and seats placed in the shrubbery walks and the grounds became a favourite place for promenading. Over the years, as fashions and needs changed, the grounds of the public park were altered and became part of a routine Parks Department bedding-out scheme, which for several summers included BRIGHTON spelled out in pansies at the entrance of what was seen as a popular seaside open space, give or take the Royal Pavilion; the paths were laid out as straight 'desire lines' to cross the town and a tarmacadamed service road led up to the front of the Pavilion, which sadly diminished the picturesque setting of the fantastic oriental building, cutting it off from the west forest lawn through which the carriages used to approach.

Following the completion of the restoration of the exterior of the Royal Pavilion in 1992 the service road has been grassed over and authentic lamp standards erected. Nash's sinuous drive, curving from the Dome and over the western lawn to the reinstated turning circle in front of the porte-cochère, has been recreated and the 'forest lawn' planting seen in his *Views of the Royal Pavilion* replaced. The instructions for planting have largely been drawn from *Sylva Florifera* of 1823, by Henry Phillips, the Brighton botanical landscape gardener, who greatly admired Aiton and the Aitonia introductions and would have watched his work at the Royal Pavilion. Some original planting lists have recently been discovered by the Director of the Royal Pavilion, which will add to the authenticity of the planting. It is most appropriate that the first major Regency garden restoration should be at Brighton, the focus for the Regency period.

Regency town planning

Regent's Park

Regent's Park in London was undoubtedly the prototype for much subsequent town planning, the ultimate and most lasting expression of the Picturesque. It was a remarkable metropolitan innovation – a royal park conceived as an extensive landscaped housing estate, the brain-child of John Nash under the patronage of the Prince Regent. A great curving thoroughfare, Regent Street, was planned to join Regent's Park to the royal heart of the capital in the Mall, St James's Palace and Park, the Regent's Carlton House, the future Buckingham Palace and, almost as an afterthought in the Prince's mind, the Palace of Westminster, the seat of government. The Regent was reported as saying that Napoleon's Paris would be eclipsed by their great new plan for London.

Marylebone Park, an area of over 500 acres (200 hectares), was originally part of Henry VIII's hunting grounds, but, unlike the other disparked London royal parks, being remote from the centre of the capital, did not become a fashionable place of recreation. Instead the Crown leased it out for farming and it was only when the last lease was about to expire that the Commissioners decided it should become a Crown housing development. Thomas Leverton, one of the architects of the Land Revenue Office, produced a scheme reminiscent of Edinburgh New Town with a series of rectangles and squares of dense housing each looking on to its own communal subscription garden.

Nash, Architect to the Office of Woods and Forests, produced a radically different scheme, which received almost instant approval in 1811. Leverton's plan was a mere gridiron extension of the neighbouring Portland estate and did nothing to check the urban sprawl by creating an open space as Nash's Marylebone, later Regent's, Park was to do; nor did it address the problem of easy access to town, which was seen as vital to attract aristocrats and professionals to a fashionable estate.

Nash seized on the idea of 'a great street' which would integrate the Marylebone estate with the centre of London and, in Prince Pückler-Muskau's words, give it 'the air of a seat of Government and not of an immeasurable metropolis of shopkeepers to use Napoleon's expression'. The bill authorising the building of Regent's Street, which was to curve like the High Street in Oxford, was passed in 1813 and, with the Prince Regent's enthusiastic support, Nash's grand scale planning could begin. The work for the

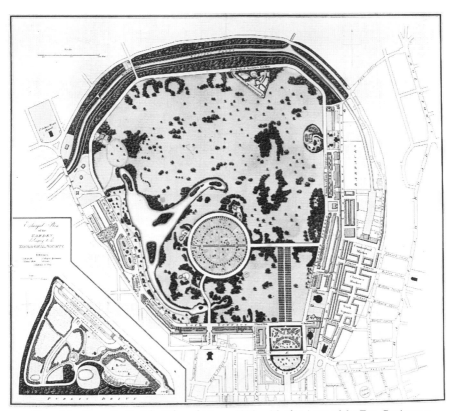

Plan of the Regent's Park by Edward Mogg, 1828, with plan inset of the Zoo. Perimeter villas and encircling canal; royal guingette removed; avenue replacing ceremonial drive through a circus, now developed into Park Square and Crescent. Zoological gardens fitted in as an 'episode'; central circus, intended for residences, earmarked for botanical garden. 'Wild wood' forest lawn planting. (Courtesy Westminster City Archives.)

Marylebone estate itself, which had already started, was to give London a new royal park.

The essential difference between the two schemes for the development of Marylebone Park that had been presented to the Commissioners was that, whereas Leverton had produced an architect's plan for a regular housing development, Nash, who had clearly profited from his five-year-long association with Repton, added the dimension of landscape gardening to the project. Repton's methods and his means of communicating ideas to his clients through illustrations in the text of the report were well-known to Nash.

These illustrations showed the scheme when finished with mature planting, which appealed to the imagination much more than a plan alone could do.

Nash's draft plan of 1811 was presented in this way with two sepia panoramas over 15 feet (4.5 metres) long showing an artist's impression of the buildings set in maturely picturesque scenery, even before the first site of the speculative venture was let and while the farmer's cows were still in possession of the fields. Repton's son, George Stanley, worked for Nash and was on hand to advise on the presentation, but, as there are notes in French, the actual drawings may have been by Augustus Pugin, the French refugee Nash had taken into his office, who was later responsible for his *Views of the Royal Pavilion.*

Villas were inset in the park, each with the setting of a country house, but in Nash's final plan, as seen laid out today, the bulk of the residential development was confined to elegant stuccoed town houses, some on a palatial scale, in perimeter terraces encircling and overlooking the park. A magnificent new church and a market service area were included. Whilst supplying a profit motive for speculative building and, bearing in mind that the Crown Commissioners were primarily interested in revenue at the expiration of the leases, Nash also recognised the need to provide a breathing space, a *rus in urbe*, and enhancement of the area for Londoners, particularly for potential wealthy clients on foot and in carriages.

Nash's draft plan was altered in the summer of 1811, after the official inauguration of the Prince as Regent, when he could take a more positive interest in the scheme. The new plan included a pleasure pavilion for the Prince Regent with on one side an ornamental canal acting as a reservoir of water for the houses, and picturesque views over the extremity of the lake on the other; this 'guingette', as it was referred to, would have been the climax of a ceremonial route from the Prince's residence at Carlton House through Regent Street, skirting Soho, and arriving at a circus before entering the royal park: a royal progress to rival Edinburgh's Royal Mile from castle to palace. The idea of the guingette was abandoned when the Prince succeeded to the throne in 1820 and Nash's energies were directed to the building of Buckingham Palace as a splendid ceremonial home for the monarch.

The Regent's Park lake, formed from the Tyburn stream, was hailed as highly successful. 'Faultless', it was pronounced by the celebrated 'parkomane', Prince Pückler-Muskau. 'You imagine you see a broad river flowing on through luxuriant banks and going off in the distance several arms; while in fact you are looking upon a

Perimeter terraces encircling and overlooking the semi-public park set a precedent for the early public park movement where middle-class housing and public amenities were linked.

small piece of standing, though clear, water created by art and labour.' It was an art learned from Repton, who in his *Sketches and Hints* had said that 'the beauty of a lake consists not so much in its size, but in those deep bays and bold promontories which prevent the eye from ranging over its whole surface'.

The secret of Nash's success in Regent's Park is that he saw it as 'one entire Park compleat in unity of character' and, although provisions were made for change of use within the original concept, he recognised that even minor changes, if uncontrolled, could be harmful. In 1821, when Decimus Burton put up Cornwall Terrace, there was a suggestion that a strip of the park opposite the houses should be surrounded by a sunk fence and be reserved for the use of the residents as the type of subscription garden, or worse still a tea garden, that Nash had been anxious to avoid. Even with restrictive covenants Nash felt that there was no permanent guarantee that there would be any control over walks, seats, planting and even ornamental pavilions serving as gardeners' tool houses. The individual planting around the park villas, on the other hand, was surrounded by plantations of forest scenery integrated with the park, so that a visitor riding round 'might recognize nothing but a park'.

Nash did appreciate, however, that there could one day be increased public accessibility to the exclusive estate and foresaw the need for some flexibility for development within the general design, if it were controlled and contained. Nash had worked with Repton at Cassiobury, where a series of different flower gardens, an American garden, a Chinese garden and a picturesque aquarium had been set in the park as 'episodes' isolated by shrubberies. The 'episodes' that developed in Regent's Park were of necessity on a larger scale than Repton's specialised gardens but the principle of discrete character areas insulated and integrated by picturesque plantations remained the same.

The most spectacular specialised garden was laid out in 1827 for the Zoological Society, under the patronage of George IV. The original request was for 20 acres (8 hectares) for 'a garden laid out in aviaries, paddocks for deer, antelopes etc' but, much to the residents' concern, lions, leopards and lynxes soon followed. William IV donated George IV's Windsor menagerie to the zoological gardens. Archery grounds were also assimilated into the park in 1832 for the Toxophilite Society and in the winter their grounds were flooded and allowed to freeze over to accommodate the London Skating Club.

The Avenue Gardens in the lower part of Broad Walk, now restored by the Royal Parks Agency to a detailed formal plan by William Andrews Nesfield of 1861, can still be said to conform to the idea of a Repton 'episode' in a landscaped garden; they are contained within the framework of the existing avenue and beyond, in the direction of the old Colosseum, is an 'English Garden' of mounded shrubberies.

In 1812 it had been suggested that there was a need for space for a botanical society. The Royal Botanic Society gardens were not achieved until 1838, however, when Robert Marnock laid out a miniature circular Regent's Park with its own specialised gardens, a rose garden, an American garden and a geographical garden insulated from each other by shrubberies. In the original plan Nash had shown a Regent's Canal to be linked with the Grand Junction Canal for easy transport of the goods to nearby markets. This would have crossed the park and provided the cheerful animation to the scenery which Repton always advocated. The Commissioners were more security-conscious about the cheerful bargemen and insisted that the Regent's Canal should go along the boundary of the park, where it would act as a bulwark against less salubrious estates.

In 1824 Nash leased the remaining land along the canal banks and built the picturesque East and West Park villages, harking back to planned Blaise Hamlet picturesque community ideas, but here, in a more upmarket situation, instead of being in vernacular cottage style, the houses were Italianate and Gothic villas, many of which were actually paired but had the appearance of one. They set a precedent for countless fringe villas in populous towns.

Regent's Park became fully open to the public in 1841 and was frequented by the fashionable classes; municipal parks soon followed the example of the royal parks to provide leisure recreation. The Avenue was laid out as gardens in 1861 by Nesfield.

Avenue Gardens: Land Use Consultants' masterplan for the restoration of Nesfield's Avenue Gardens by the Royal Parks Agency.

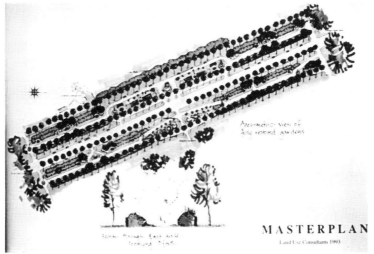

Axonometric view of fully restored gardens

MASTERPLAN

Land Use Consultants 1993

Nash's Park Village; reminiscent of the layout of his early Blaise Hamlet.

Regent's Park as the prototype of Regency town planning

Regent's Park, with its Picturesque inspiration, had broken the eighteenth-century mould of the geometry of the Edinburgh New Town and the Bath town planning. Although the elderly Nash drew up a plan for Leamington Spa in 1827 and went down to the new Regent's Hotel to supervise the start of work, little of his plan appears to have been carried out. It was his close Regent's Park associates, James Burton and his son Decimus, trained by Nash, who carried through his vision for town planning in St Leonards in Sussex and Tunbridge Wells in Kent. They also contributed ideas for a new Brighton, although it was the architects Charles Busby and Amon Wilds and the landscape gardener Henry Phillips who were responsible for the layouts of the new fashionable suburbs in Regency Brighton.

James Burton had been essential to the planning of Regent's Park as he promoted the speculative buildings and built most of the houses in the Nash terraces himself. His son, Decimus, built several of the Park villas, including the Holme, the Burtons' own house. Decimus Burton proved a lively and versatile architect- planner; he was appointed architect for the Regent's Park zoo and built a number of the villa conservatories. His most notable achievement in conservatory domes, built twenty years before his famous Palm House at Kew, was the Colosseum on the eastern side of Regent's Park in 1824.

The Holme was Regent's Park's earliest villa, built in 1817 for the Burton family by the young Decimus.

The Colosseum, which soon attracted London's most fashionable society, housed a giant panorama of the city under its vast dome; the conservatories were entered by a subterranean passage of interconnected compartments, which formed a promenade in the manner of Repton's proposed enfilade flower corridor for the Brighton Pavilion. There was also an underground marine grotto and a Swiss cottage. Decimus Burton's Colosseum, built in iron and glass with unsupported spans and curved surfaces, was trend-setting and opened up new possibilities for menageries and tropical plant collections.

In 1825 Henry Phillips conceived for Brighton the idea of an 'oriental garden' inside a vast domed conservatory, but, instead of being classical like Burton's Colosseum, in a style of architecture in keeping with the Brighton Pavilion. The steam-heated conservatory was to have been called the Athenaeum and to have housed tropical plants; it would have included a library, museum and an institute where Phillips hoped to lecture. In the event he could not raise the money and the venture is remembered only by Oriental Place, which was to link the Athenaeum to the sea. Undeterred, Phillips built an even larger conservatory further west in Hove in 1832, to be called the Antheum, for exotic birds and trees with an amphitheatre to seat eight hundred. This collapsed just before it was due to be opened and a gardener, who was the only person in the building at the time, had a miraculous escape.

The German Spa, with floriferous shrubbery walks, opened under royal patronage in 1825, as part of Brighton's Regency attractions.

Two other Regent's Park ventures to fail in Brighton were the Royal Zoological Garden by Matthew Wyatt and the Decimus Burton project of Furze Hill, to the north of the present Adelaide Crescent, which was planned in a circular way in the manner of Regent's Park, with individual, different-style houses like those in Nash's Park Villages. Kemp Town, to the east of Brighton, in 1823 and Brunswick Square, to the west, in 1824 were successful, however, and remain as outstanding examples of Regency town planning.

Kemp Town enclosures

Kemp Town, in 1823, was a new social experiment. Brighton had developed as a seaside resort from a fishing village and, with the fame, or notoriety, that the Prince Regent had given it, had greatly expanded, becoming distinctly crowded in the season. Kemp Town, like Regent's Park, was conceived as a spacious new fashionable grand scale residential estate; it was not a seaside resort such as Jane Austen had described in *Sanditon* in 1817, one of the many Sussex 'rising Bathing-Places' starting up by the sea with 'a little Crescent', usually called Waterloo, and coming to nothing. Kemp Town was a success story as more and more people wanted to live by the sea, which was more romantic than the once popular inland spa. It was Thomas Read Kemp MP who had originally conceived the idea of erecting an estate on his land to the east of Brighton which, in spite of early financial difficulties and some curtailment to the original plan, was laid out by Amon Wilds and Charles Busby as a co-ordinated whole. It had the great advantage of being a sloping site looking out on to the sea.

Henry Phillips, the botanical landscape gardener, who wrote *Sylva Florifera* in 1823, had already, with Henry Kendall the surveyor, laid out and planted the enclosures when the first meeting of the proprietors took place in 1828; it was presumably their plan, claimed by the Brighton papers to have 'great novelty and beauty of style', which was entered on a local map of that date. The mounds that Phillips created for increased privacy and for protection for the plants from the sea breezes remain today. Thomas Cubitt, who built thirty-seven of the 106 houses and himself lived at 13 Lewes Crescent, was appointed 'to superintend the general works and improvements'.

A new piece of Regency seaside social history was the subterranean passage from the Kemp Town subscription gardens to the lower level of the Esplanade entrance, built by Kendall, which was flanked by two cottages, one for the gardener and one for the constable; at a still lower level down the planted slopes was a residents' reading

The elegant Regency layout proposed for Kemp Town, which was not completely carried out.

Kemp Town: elegant Regency terraces, a crescent and a square began to be built in 1823 by Thomas Kemp with gardens laid out by Henry Phillips.

room, where parents could read the newspapers while their children were taken to bathing machines below. The Duke of Devonshire was an early resident of Kemp Town, with the most favoured site overlooking the sea and gardens, and there is a tradition that he brought his head gardener from Chatsworth, Joseph Paxton, to advise on the laying out of the Slopes; he may well have collaborated with Phillips on other aspects of planting of the garden enclosures.

Three names known to have been associated with the actual laying out and management of the Kemp Town enclosures, Kemp, Kendall and Cubitt, reappear in connection with Belgrave Square in London, begun in 1826 by Thomas Cubitt as part of the Grosvenor estate. Kemp had a house in the south-west corner built by Kendall. Not surprisingly an engraving of the square in 1827 shows planting in progress very similar to that in the Kemp Town enclosure.

Patterned shrubberies gave a more structured design than informal 'forest lawn' planting within the geometrical enclosures, dictated by squares and crescents. The new look can be seen at Park Square in Nash's plan for Regent's Park and in his plan for Leamington. Although the Kemp Town plan for patterned shrubberies appears to look formal, untrimmed shrubs gave informality to the design, if planted in the floriferous way Phillips recommended in his book.

St James's Park and Buckingham Palace

John Nash was 75 when he embarked on the final stage of George IV's grand architectural programme to make London fit for the British monarchy. Buckingham House, where King George III and

Queen Charlotte had lived modestly, was to be transformed into a palace with the Mall revamped as a ceremonial approach road with a triumphal Marble Arch in celebration of Waterloo, a copy of the arch of Constantine in Rome, at the entrance to the new grand palace. Carlton House could then be demolished in 1827 and replaced by an elegant terrace of town houses as a backdrop to the Mall. St James's Park, laid out with public walks beside a naturalised lake, would complement the scenes and provide picturesque viewing points for Nash's spectacular new Regency architecture.

St James's Park as left by George III still had the formal canal laid out by Charles II and the public was confined to a perimeter walk. 'Capability' Brown's plan for St James's Park resembled any other of his country house layouts with smooth lawns and clumped trees but Nash set out to cater for the public, covering the grass with shaped mounds and shrubbery walks for perambulation. The straight canal was converted into a lake with irregular margins and an island formed at each end; the lower one was named, after Charles II's duck decoy, Duck Island, on which in 1837 a picturesque Birdkeeper's Lodge was built for the Ornithological Society.

The term used in Nash's contract was the forming of 'ornamental shrubberies', which by the late 1820s had a specific meaning: the *Sylva Florifera* described by Henry Phillips. Fortunately, Pückler-

Plan of St James's Park, 1829. Prince Pückler-Muskau saw the ornamental shrubberies being planted and copied them on his estate.

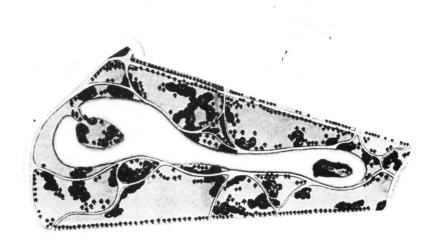

Duck Island with Birdkeeper's Lodge showing Nash's mounded shrubberies round the lake and his Marble Arch (removed in 1851) in front of Buckingham Palace.

Muskau was on hand daily while in London in 1829 with his note-taking gardener and watched the shrubberies being staked out and planted, admiring the combination of untrimmed shrubs and flowers as in all 'wild wood and shrub plantations'. In his *Hints on Landscape Gardening*, published in 1834, he produced a diagram to show how to plant an ornamental shrubbery, with flowering shrubs and hardy perennials, having lamented that at Muskau he could not enjoy the range of shrubs that he saw growing in England.

Nash and W. T. Aiton

Pückler Muskau had paid several visits to Nash, to whom he said he was indebted for 'much valuable instruction in my art', but it was undoubtedly Aiton who provided the floriferous element to Nash's ornamental gardening, when after 1820 he was able to use his services as royal gardener. Nash had used only tree plantations with some shrubs in Regent's Park and when, in 1817, he was asked to design a layout for St James's Square, which would transform it from a baroque square into a picturesque garden, his shrubberies contained no flowers.

Aiton and his father, who were much respected by the royal family, both worked at Frogmore, where they would have planted the influential Mason-inspired flower garden for Queen Charlotte. Having been responsible for the Kew gardens over a long period of time, their main interest was in botany and horticulture. Aiton's 1813 revision of his father's five-volumed *Hortus Kewensis* provides the most comprehensive catalogue of plants available in the Regency.

In 1820, when W. T. Aiton was elevated to the position of Director General of His Majesty's Gardens, he was frequently called to Royal

Lodge at Windsor. He also joined Nash at Brighton and there and later in St James's Park and Buckingham Palace they perfected the type of ornamental shrubbery in which Nash indicated the shapes, ground formation and paths and Aiton was responsible for the floriferous planting, often using plants from Kew, where he worked with Sir Joseph Banks.

Fig 24 : Two views interpreting the visual effect of planting from the plan by Prince Pückler-Muskau (Fig 25) of the method according to John Nash (in Andeutungen über Landschaftsgärtnerei). The outline of the bed is with bays and promontaries and the shrubs and herbaceous plants are grouped in masses which unite.

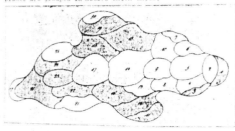

A diagram of a Nash-type ornamental shrubbery from Hermann Pückler-Muskau's 'Hints on Landscape Gardening' with perspective planting plan interpreted by Mark Laird.

Loudon and the wind of change

The ideas that would culminate, two years after the death of George IV, in the Reform Act of 1832, had already begun to take root alongside the extravagant fantasy of the Brighton Pavilion, Repton's Red Books and the genteel world of Jane Austen's novels. The other more restless world of rick burning and Peterloo, in a changing landscape of enclosure and the growth of towns, was depicted in 1821 in *Rural Rides* by William Cobbett, the mouthpiece of popular reform.

J. C. Loudon paralleled Cobbett's agitation for social and political reform by a campaign for public environmental improvements. Loudon began his career as a landscape gardener with private commissions but soon extended his landscaping ideas into provisions for public parks, open spaces, town squares, cemeteries, a green belt for the metropolis, botanic gardens and arboreta. By 1822, when Loudon published his *Encyclopaedia of Gardening*, he was fired by a crusading zeal for horticultural education, particularly

Great Tew, Oxfordshire; from J. C. Loudon's 'Observations on laying out Farms in the Scotch style adapted to England', 1812, which demonstrated his utilitarian ideas for landscape husbandry.

for villa and suburban gardening, and in 1826 founded his *Gardener's Magazine*.

Loudon's first book, *Observations on the Formation and Management of Useful and Ornamental Plantations* in 1804, was dedicated to the King but brought him no royal patronage. The inclusion of 'useful and ornamental' in the title of the book was an early indication of Loudon's utilitarian aesthetics. He had met Jeremy Bentham that year and became a lifelong admirer and follower of his guiding principle of 'the greatest happiness of the greatest number'. Loudon felt that a landscape gardener had an important role to play in promoting utilitarianism and advocated a liberal education with a knowledge of agriculture, botany, architecture and gardening. Loudon's next book, *A Treatise on Forming, Improving and Managing Country Residences*, published in 1806, set out his creed of 'a taste founded in Nature with Economy and Utility'.

Landscape husbandry: Great Tew, Oxfordshire

Loudon studied agriculture in Edinburgh and in 1808, after the publication of a pamphlet on Scottish farming, General Stratton, the landlord of Great Tew, invited him to manage his 1800 acre (728 hectare) estate in an effort to increase wartime food production.

Loudon was still only twenty-five and the Tew estate was wonderful land-use training for a young man bent on environmental planning. He had 132 workers under him and complete control over the planning of roads, drainage, fences, buildings and plantations. At Tew Lodge, where he took up residence, he set up a training college where the sons of landed proprietors could study farming techniques. From the verandah of Regency Tew Lodge he could look out over Reptonian flower baskets on to the farm, with a speaking trumpet and French horn to hand to shout instructions.

Loudon saw his work essentially as landscape gardening in the eighteenth-century tradition but adapted to utilitarian principles as 'landscape husbandry' or 'rural scenery', which combined agriculture and gardening. He used the same landscape components of water, trees and beautiful landforms, but the water also served the useful purpose of a reservoir for the threshing machine and for flooding in case of fire; the serpentined lanes reflected the line of Beauty, but following the contours made the passage of the dung carts up the hill easier. Temples and rustic summerhouses could still be erected for the enjoyment of prospects but looking out over good Oxfordshire redlands and thriving crops rather than on to idealised landscape.

The most fertile parts of the estate were planted with crops and the less fertile slopes carried the ornamental plantations. So advanced was Loudon's thinking that he even stressed ecological considerations such as the advantages of hedgerows and wedge planting to shelter wild life. Farm buildings fitted snugly into the landscape and the village was improved, not as a village ornée like Old Warden, but as a landlord's village where the vernacular cottages were given neat small front gardens, and quarter-acre strips for cultivation at the back.

From private to public parks

Loudon saw the public park as a major instrument of social reform, 'to afford a free wholesome air', as early as 1822, when he wrote his *Encyclopaedia of Gardening*. It was not until the post-Reform Act Select Committee on Public Walks in 1833 pronounced that 'the spring to industry which occasional relaxation gives, seems quite as necessary to the poor as to the rich' that steps were taken to acquire spaces for open-air recreation. In London only the royal parks were open to the public but in 1840 a new public royal park was authorised in the east end of London, to be called Victoria Park. The park, which was at the eastern end of the Regent's Canal, was laid out by James Pennethorne, Mary Ann Nash's adopted son and Nash's pupil. The design was in the best tradition of landscaped

Victoria Park, east London, which, following Regent's Park and St James's Park, was designed as public walks in a picturesque landscaped park.

parks with a lake made from a gravel pit and to the delights of ornamental garden buildings, such as a pagoda on an island, more popular playground features were added.

Public parks with the same objectives of providing fresh air for those who lived in crowded conditions sprang up all over Britain, provided not, as with Victoria Park, by Act of Parliament but by local philanthropists. It was fitting that Loudon was asked to design the earliest of these in 1840, the Derby Arboretum, donated by the philanthropist, Joseph Strutt. Loudon, who had just published his eight-volume *Arboretum et Fruticetum Britannicum*, had decided on an arboretum, for education and recreation, with all trees labelled, 'to excite an interest in the subject of trees and shrubs in the minds of general observers'.

Birkenhead Park, designed by Joseph Paxton and opened in 1847, was internationally famous and claimed to be the first municipal park, financed by the people for the people. Its quality much impressed F. L. Olmsted, who visited it eight years before he designed Central Park, Manhattan. Olmsted, who was much influenced by A. J. Downing and by Loudon's utilitarian ideas, wrote of Birkenhead Park: 'I was ready to admit that in Democratic America, there was nothing to be thought comparable with this People's Garden. Indeed, gardening had here reached a Perfection that I had never dreamed of...nor merely was the Park beautiful, it was useful...all this magnificent pleasure ground is entirely, unreservedly and for ever the people's own.'

Southampton's green lungs are possibly a direct result of Loudon's campaigning in his *Hints for Breathing Places for the Metropolis*, which resulted in 1837 in a House of Commons resolution that all future enclosure bills should include provisions for public open space. Loudon had stayed a month in Southampton when he was asked to plan the town cemetery and in 1843 gave 'Hints for Improvement of the Town of Southampton'. At a time when a series of commons were being enclosed, it was first thought that a Regent's Park with inset villas should be built, but in 1844, after enclosure, the commons were dedicated as open spaces and converted into public parks. Philip Brannon's view of Southampton Park resembles Loudon's gardenesque plan for the pleasure grounds of Coleshill, a latterday private commission in 1843 for the radical Earl of Radnor, a close friend of Bentham and Cobbett.

The gardenesque

J. C. Loudon died in 1843 and had by then evolved a new system of landscape improvement, called the gardenesque, which was itself soon to be eclipsed by Victorian gardening. It was in 1832 that Loudon appropriated the word gardenesque in his influential *Gardener's*

Southampton Parks: watercolour by Philip Brannon, based on a Loudon gardenesque vision of green lungs created out of the enclosure of the commons in 1846. (Courtesy of Southampton City Art Gallery.)

Magazine, giving it the meaning 'as a gardener would like', in the same way as picturesque had been used to mean 'as a painter would like'. Loudon was not the only one who felt that horticulture had been neglected in the cult of the Picturesque and, as early as 1805, the Horticultural Society of London (later the Royal Horticultural Society) was formed. At their first meeting it was regretted that there was a lack of scientific information about horticultural matters, particularly the selection of good forms of plants and their cultivation.

All Loudon's training and inclinations were scientific and, with a slogan and a flag to fly, the great educator went all out for a gardenesque style, which was calculated 'to display the individual beauty of trees, shrubs and plants in a state of nature'. As a botanist, Loudon found increasingly that horticulture and the 'scenery of Nature', particularly the forest lawn planting he once advocated, were at variance. Gardening was an art and science, not to be left to the vagaries of nature. Careful consideration should be given to the needs of the plant in terms of light and space, pruning, grading for height in the shrubbery, mounded scenery to display plants; no more picturesque intertwinings, recessing of plants, nor scattering of grass seed in the shrubbery to make it look as though it grew naturally on a forest lawn.

Loudon did not believe in a battle of styles, however, and never lost sight of the principles of landscape gardening. He intended to reprint with notes the works of Shenstone, Whately, Mason, Gilpin, Price and Repton, but in the event he managed to publish only Repton's. In the Preface to Repton's works he stated that the aim of the gardenesque was 'to add to the acknowledged charms of the Repton school all those which the sciences of gardening and botany, in their present advanced state are capable of producing'. Loudon was in his element in his plan for the Birmingham Botanic Garden, where he could blend 'scientific arrangement with picturesque effect'.

As Victoria's reign progressed new garden designs appeared which adhered to the principles of neither the picturesque nor the gardenesque. The abolition of the tax on glass in 1845 brought the greenhouse within the means of most garden owners and the introduction of half-hardy plants from all over the world gave new dimensions to horticulture, particularly in summer bedding. The more subtle, graceful, ornamental Regency gardening was forgotten in the proliferation of shows, carpet bedding and the architectural flower gardens of Nesfield and Barry with their dazzling displays of colour and pattern.

Cruikshank's satirical view of the new craze for horticulture, which would sound the death knell for Regency ornamental gardening.

Further reading

Batey, Mavis, and Lambert, David. *The English Garden Tour*. John Murray, 1990.

Boniface, Priscilla. *In Search of English Gardens: The Travels of J. C. Loudon*. Lennard Publishing, 1987.

Carter, George; Goode, Patrick; and Laurie, Kedrun. *Humphry Repton Landscape Gardener*. Victoria and Albert Museum, 1983.

Conner, Patrick. *Oriental Architecture in the West*. Thames & Hudson, 1979.

Elliott, Brent. *Victorian Gardens*. Batsford, 1986.

Garden History (the Journal of the Garden History Society), 22, 2 (1994). Special Picturesque issue.

Jacques, David. *Georgian Gardens*. Batsford, 1983.

Morley, John. *Regency Design*. Zwemmer, 1993.

Nash, John. *Views of the Brighton Pavilion*. Republished by Pavilion, 1991.

Picturesque Exhibition catalogue. Hereford, 1994.

Pückler-Muskau, Hermann. *Regency Visitor*. 1957.

Pückler-Muskau, Hermann. *Puckler's Progress*. Collins, 1987.

Saunders, Ann. *Regent's Park*. Bedford College, London, 1981.

Simo, Melanie. *Loudon and the Landscape*. 1988.

Strong, Roy. *Royal Gardens*. Hecote, 1993.

Stroud, Dorothy. *Humphry Repton*. Country Life, 1962.

Summerson, John. *John Nash*. 1980.

Tait, A.A. *The Landscape Garden in Scotland 1735-1835*. Edinburgh University Press, 1980.

Temple, Nigel. *John Nash and the Village Picturesque*. A. J. Sutton, 1979.

Some Regency sites to visit

Public open spaces

Blaise Castle, near Bristol, Avon. Grounds with Nash dairy.

Blaise Hamlet, near Bristol, Avon. (National Trust.) Access to village green but not to cottages.

Brunswick Square, Hove, East Sussex.

Crescent Garden, Alverstoke, Gosport, Hampshire.

Derby Arboretum, Derby.

Kemp Town, Brighton, East Sussex. Gardens of the Regency crescent and square visible but no access.

Regent's Park, London NW1.

St James's Park, London SW1.

Southampton central parks, Hampshire.

Sydney Gardens, Bath, Avon.

Victoria Park, London E9.

Virginia Water, Sunningdale, Berkshire.

Houses and gardens

Ashridge, Berkhamsted, Hertfordshire HP4 1NS. Telephone: 01442 843491.

Audley End House and Park, Saffron Walden, Essex CB11 4JF. (English Heritage.) Telephone: 01799 522399.

Drummond Castle Gardens, Muthill, Crieff, Perthshire PH5 2AA. Telephone: 01764 681257.

Endsleigh House, Milton Abbot, near Tavistock, Devon PL19 0PQ. Telephone: 01822 87248. Swiss Cottage (Landmark Trust).

Houghton Lodge Gardens, Stockbridge, Hampshire SO20 6LQ. Telephone: 01264 810177 or 810502.

Keats House, Wentworth Place, Keats Grove, Hampstead, London NW3 3RR. Telephone: 0171-435 2062.

Leigh Park, Havant, Hampshire. Telephone: 01705 451540.

Mount Edgcumbe House and Park, Cremyll, Torpoint, Cornwall PL10 1HZ. Telephone: 01752 822236.

Pitshanger Manor, Mattock Lane, Ealing, London W5 5EQ. Telephone: 0181-567 1227.

Royal Pavilion, Brighton, East Sussex BN1 1UE. Telephone: 01273 603005.

Sezincote, Moreton-in-Marsh, Gloucestershire GL56 9AW.

Strawberry Hill, Waldegrave Road, Twickenham, Middlesex TW1 4SX. Telephone: 0181-892 0051.

The Swiss Garden, Old Warden, near Biggleswade, Bedfordshire. Telephone: 01234 228330.

Windsor Castle, Windsor, Berkshire SL4 1NJ. Telephone: 01753 868286.

Index

Page numbers in italic type refer to illustrations

Abbotsford 56
Ackermann, Rudolph 6, *16*, *26*, *34*, 36, 37
Addison, Joseph 5
Adlestrop *13*, 14
Aiton, William 84
Aiton, William Townsend 6, 43, 58, 64, 70, 71, 84, 85
Alderson, Christopher 53
Alton Towers 40
Alverstoke: Crescent Garden 47-8, *49*
Ashridge 20, *52*, 54
Audley End *57*, 58
Austen, Jane 5, 10, 13, 19, 22, 29, 48, 86
Banks, Joseph 42, 85
Barry, Charles 92
Bateman, Dickie 48
Bath 78; *see also* Sydney Gardens
Beckford, William 20
Belgrave Square 82
Bentham, Jeremy 87
Birkenhead Park 90
Birmingham Botanic Garden 92
Blaise Castle *11*, 14
Blaise Hamlet *12*, 14, 76
Bonomi, Joseph 9
Brannon, Phillip 90
Brighton 59, *80*; *see also* Kemp Town, Royal Pavilion
Brislington House *41*
Brown, Lancelot 5, 65, 83
Buckingham Palace 70, 72, 74, 82
Burke, Edmund 5
Burlington, 3rd Earl of 5
Burton, Decimus 75, 78, 79, 80
Burton, James 78
Busby, Charles 81
Byron, George Gordon 59
Carlton House 36, 67, 68, 69, 72, 74, 83
Cassiobury 76
Chambers, William 37
Charlotte, Queen 53, 67, 69, 83
Cheltenham 1
Clark, Frank 54
Claude Lorrain 7, 8
Cobbett, William 86
Cockerell, Charles 62
Cockerell, Samuel Pepys 62
Coleridge, Samuel Taylor 68, 69
Coleshill 90
Colosseum 79
Craven Cottage 35
Cruikshank, George 92
Cubitt, Thomas 81, 82
Daniell, Thomas and William 59, *60*, 62, 66, 68
Davis, Alexander 33
Derby Arboretum 90
Downing, Andrew Jackson 6, *32*, 33-5, 45, 90
Downton Castle *2*, *3*, 7, 8, 19
Drummond Castle 56, *57*
East Cowes Castle *64*
Edgeworth, Maria 23
Edinburgh 55, 56, 72, 87

Endsleigh *13*, 15, 40
Fish, Thomas 29
Fitzherbert, Maria 59, 65, 68
Fonthill *18*, 70
Fortune, Robert 42
Frogmore 53, 84
Furze Hill 80
George III 36, 82, 83, 87
George IV (also Prince of Wales and Regent) *4*, 5, 29, 35, 36,*3* 7, 55, 58, 59-71, 86
Gilpin, William 43, 44, 45, 46, 49, 55, 70, 92
Gilpin, William Sawrey 6, 45, 58
Goldsmith, Oliver 10, 11
Goodwin, Francis 22
Great Tew *86*, *87*, 88
Hafod 53-4
Harcourt, 1st Earl 10, 11
Harcourt, 2nd Earl 44, 49
Harford, John Scandrett 14
Hearne, Thomas 8
Hesse-Homburg, Duchess of 36
Hluboka *56*
Hogarth, William 5
Holland, Henry 59
Hopper, Thomas 35, 36
Houghton 9
Hove 79, 80
Jellicoe, Geoffrey 67
Johnes, Thomas 53
Johnson, Samuel 10
Keats, John 25
Keats House *24*, 25-6
Kemp, Thomas Read 80
Kemp Town 43, 80, *81*, *82*
Kendall, Henry 81, 82
Kennedy, Lewis 56, 58
Kerr, William 71
Kew 59, 62, 71, 78, 85
Knight, Richard Payne 7, 8, 19, 33, 55
Knowle Cottage *27*, 28
Laird, Mark *85*
Land Use Consultants *77*
Lapidge, Samuel 65
Leamington 78, 82
Leigh Park *16*, 17, 39, 41-2, 66
Leverton, Thomas 72, 73
Lieven, Princess *4*, 36, 69
Little Horsted 67
Loudon, Jane 33
Loudon, John Claudius 6, 32, 33, 46, *47*, 48, 53, 56, 66, 70, 86-92
Lugar, Robert 9
Luscombe *7*, 8
Macartney, George 42
Malton, James 8, 9
Marnock, Robert 76
Martin, John 62, 63
Mason, William 44, 48, 49, 53, 54, 70, 92
Matlock *19*, 20
McCarthy, John 69
Melrose Abbey 56
Montgomery Place 33, *34*, 35

Mount Edgcumbe *53*, 54, *55*
Nash, John 6, 7, 14, 43, 65, 67, 68, 70, 71, 72, 88
Nesfield, William Andrews 76, *83*, 92
New Forest 43, 44, *45*
Nuneham Courtenay 9, *10*, 11, 44, 48, *49*
Old Warden 88; *see also* Swiss Garden
Old Windsor 48
Olmsted, Frederick Law 90
Ongley, 3rd Lord 40
Osborne, Wendy 48
Owen, Thomas Ellis 54
Oxford *see* Worcester College
Papworth, John Buonarotti 6, 22, 37, *38*, 40, 42
Paxton, Joseph 82, 90
Pennethorne, James 88
Phillips, Henry 6, 43, 46 ,47, 71, 79, 81, 82, 83
Pitshanger Manor 23, 24
Plas Newydd 35
Plaw, John 15, 17, 37
Pope, Alexander 5
Porden,William 59, 65
Porter, Walsh 35
Poussin, Nicholas 7
Price, Uvedale 7, 8, 11, 14, 37, 40, 45, 55, 58, 70, 92
Pückler-Muskau, Hermann von 6, 14, 23, 36, 58, 72, 74, 83, 85
Pugin, Augustus 74
Regent's Park 72, *73*, 74, *75*, 76, *77*, *78*, 79
Repton, Humphry 5, 6, 7, 14, 15, *21*, 22, 26, 27, 29, 31, 33, 42, *52*, 53, 54, 59, 60, 62-8, 73, 75, 76, 79, 88, 92
Repton, John Stanley and George Adey 14, 15, 74
Richardson, Samuel 22
Robertson, W. 26
Robinson, Peter Frederick 40, 63
Rogers, Samuel 59
Rousseau, Jean Jacques 49, 53
Royal Horticultural Society 70, 91
Royal Parks Agency 76
Royal Pavilion, Brighton 6, 43, 59-71, *61*, *64*, *67*, *69*, 86
St James's Park 43, 70, 82, *83*, *84*
St James's Square 84
St Leonards 78
Sandby, Paul 48, 49

Sandby, Thomas 36
Scotney Castle 6
Scott, Walter 55, 56
Sezincote 42, 62, *63*
Shaftesbury, 3rd Earl of 5
Shenstone, William 17, 92
Sidmouth 20; *see also* Knowle Cottage, Woolbrook Cottage
Soane, Sir John 23, 24, 28, 56
Southampton 90, *91*
Southcote, Philip 17, 48
Southey, Robert 53, 56
Staunton, Sir George 41, 42, 66
Stoke Farm, Bucks *16*, 17
Stoke Park 53
Stoneleigh Abbey 5, *12*, 22, 29, *30*, *31*
Stratton, G. F 87
Strawberry Hill *18*, 19, 20
Strutt, Joseph 90
Swiss Garden 37, *38*, *40*, *41*
Sydney Gardens, Bath 43, *49*
Torquay *see* Woodbine Cottage
Tunbridge Wells 78
Valleyfield, Fife *60*
Victoria, Queen 71
Victoria Park 88, 89, 90
Virginia Water *35*, 36, 42, 70
Walpole, Horace 19, 20, 48
Watteau,Antoine 29, 66
West Cottage *17*, 19
Whately, Thomas 92
White, Gilbert 48
Whitehead, William 11
Whiteknights 41
Wilds, Amon 81
Windsor: Castle 58; Royal Lodge *34*, 35, 36, 68, 70, 84; *see also* Frogmore, Virginia Water
Woburn Abbey 5, 14, 28, 42
Woburn Farm 48
Woodbine Cottage, Torquay *8*
Woolbrook Cottage, Sidmouth *20*
Worcester College, Oxford 43, *44*
Wordsworth, William 14
Wright, Thomas 48
Wyatt, James 19, 20
Wyatville, Sir Jeffry 15, 35, 36, 37, 40, 58

ACKNOWLEDGEMENTS

Warmest thanks to George Carter, Russell Cleaver , Jane Crawley, Ray Desmond, Alistair Forsyth, Richard Flenley, Hazel Fryer, Peter Goodchild, Keith Goodway, Virginia Hinze, Fiona Jamieson, Mark Laird, David Lambert, Thomas Lloyd, Wendy Osborne, Stella Palmer, Pamela Paterson, Jessica Rutherford, Ann Saunders, Timothy Steinhoff, Michael Symes, Nigel Temple, Marion Waller. A DNH grant for Information Files is gratefully acknowledged.

Photographs are reproduced by courtesy of the following: Hazel Conway, page 89; Hazel Fryer, page 27; Keith Goodway, page 64; Lady Pamela Hicks, page 51 (top); Virginia Hinze, page 60; Fiona Jamieson, page 57; Alun Jones, page 86; Mark Laird, page 85; David Lambert, page 35; Land Use Consultants, page 77 (both); Thomas Lloyd, page 8; London Gardens Trust, page 84; Dodie Masterman, page 80; Wendy Osborne, page 49 (lower); Stella Palmer, pages 13, 38, 60; Pitshanger Manor Museum, page 24 (top); Staunton Country Park, pages 16, 39.

We are particularly grateful to Brighton Borough Council and Leisure Services for allowing us to use their photographs of the Royal Pavilion for pages 4, 61, 64 (lower) and for the cover.